HOW TO USE
THE POWER OF
SELF-HYPNOSIS

Shows you how to break tiresome habits caused
by anxiety, depression or lack of self-confidence.

HOW TO USE
THE POWER OF SELF-HYPNOSIS

JUSUF HARIMAN
M.A., Ph.D., M.I.A.A.Ps.

THORSONS

THORSONS PUBLISHING GROUP

First published 1981
This edition 1988

© JUSUF HARIMAN 1981

British Library Cataloguing in Publication Data

Hariman, Jusuf
How to use the power of self-hypnosis.
1. Autogenic training
I. Title
154.7'6   RC499.S/

ISBN 0-7225-1570-7

*Published by Thorsons Publishers Limited, Wellingborough,
Northamptonshire, NN8 2RQ, England*

Printed in Great Britain by Richard Clay Limited, Bungay, Suffolk

3 5 7 9 10 8 6 4 2

Contents

Dedication

This book is dedicated to my parents who have given me so much. Without their love and care I would not have been able to do what I have done.

Acknowledgements

My greatest debt is to the many writers I have read and the many speakers I have heard, all of whom have stimulated me to learn how to build a better life.

Special thanks are due to Michael Grassan for his encouragement, and to *Good Health* magazine for permission to use material from some of my previously published articles.

I am grateful to my Ph.D. supervisor, Dr Les Carr from Columbia Pacific University for his kind thoughts and support, and to my good friend Dr Philip Smith, whose constant faith in me during difficult times can be likened to a light in the darkness.

Without doubt the strongest and steadiest help has come from my wife Polly. Her thoughtful comments and her patience formed an environment in which the whole thing became possible.

ACKNOWLEDGEMENTS

Preface

You are what you will yourself to be. In that great kingdom of
the mind, you fashion in the precious mould of thoughts, the
motive power which shapes your destiny. For what you think
is what you will become, what you believe in indicates the way,
and whilst you live, the will is never dumb. Remember when
your life you plan, it has been sagely said of man, this I can if I
think I can.

Anonymous

The strategies taught in this book are derived from my
practical experience of everyday clinical interaction between
myself and my clients and students, even though I have
indicated their general application by citing from and
pointing to the works of well known professionals in this field.
Far from being a mere speculation, they are dictated by what
experience has shown to be effective, workable and beneficial.
Some testimonies to this effect are included verbatim in
Chapter 15.

Although short, these strategies represent the essence of tips
or instructions which a good clinical hypnotherapist can be
expected to give to his clients. The book is intended to be a
short encyclopedia of 'problems of living', and it is aimed at
those whose problems lie between *mild* and *almost severe*. If your
problem exceeds this limit (i.e. severe or very severe), then you
would be well advised to seek the guidance of a qualified
professional.

If you have a variety of problems, I suggest you construct a
list of priorities and then handle them one by one in order of
importance. What typically happens in this case is that as one
really masters a certain problem, other problems
automatically decrease in strength and become easier to
handle. Psychologists sometimes call it the 'generalisation
effect'.

In order to benefit fully from this book, it is essential that
you read and understand thoroughly Chapters 1, 2 and 3.
Chapters 1 and 2 will give you a correct understanding of

hypnosis, and in Chapter 1 a model for the effective use of self-hypnosis is given. In Chapter 3, the concrete use of the model is given for the first time in the book, and throughout, frequent reference will be made to this chapter.

1.

What Is Hypnosis?

The hypnotic trance is essentially a state of deep absorption. During hypnosis a good hypnotic subject is deeply interested in whatever the operator is saying. He steadfastly concentrates on his instructions and holds them fast before his mind. In case conflicting ideas come to consciousness, he may bring his will-power into play, to exclude the irrelevant idea, so that the idea imparted by the hypnotist becomes the sole idea in his mind.

Pursuing the matter further, Dr C. Leuba from Antioch College, U.S.A., asserts that 'the essence of hypnosis consists in creating a willingness and an ability, especially on the part of the person in whom ideomotor action is strong and imagery vivid, to concentrate exclusively on the situations, concrete or symbolic, which the hypnotist presents to him.'

This conception of hypnosis is consistent with the well-known spontaneous occurrence of hypnotic-like states in daily life, as when one is deeply absorbed. To quote Dr D. Coleman,

> We all undergo everyday trances from time to time, when we are pre-occupied with what we are doing. In these moments we are oblivious to what happens around us. The football fan watching the grand final on TV for example, is fully alert to the game, but unaware of his body sitting in the chair or his wife calling him to dinner.

Other phenomena have been mentioned by Dr Leuba,

> When reality is very harsh and people withdraw from it to concentrate exclusively on their own more pleasant imaginings, and become oblivious of their surroundings, their imaginings are

likely to take on the reality of those under hypnosis; they become hallucinations. All of us, too, have been analgesic at times; while absorbed in the detective story we may lose awareness of the toothache or other painful stimulation, or when similarly absorbed we may be temporarily deaf, as we fail to hear the door bell or a question directed to us. We have all also been hypersensitive at times as we expected and concentrated on the pain from the dentist's drill or an unpleasant taste or smell. All of us, too, have been unable at times to carry out a really simple and easy action as we became convinced that we could not do it. As soon as we concentrated on not being able to jump across the two foot chasm or the puddle of dirty water we were rooted to the spot and really could not jump across it. But the moment our confidence was re-established and we thought exclusively of performing the action successfully, we could easily do it. All these phenomena, as also the amnesias of everyday life, such as forgetting a well known name, are commonplace.

Dispelling a Few Myths

Under close scrutiny, the 'concentration' view of hypnosis also serves to dispel the most prevalent myths about hypnosis, since it implies the following important points.

1. Hypnosis Is Not Sleep

As Dr Herbert Spiegel, Clinical Professor of Psychiatry at Columbia's College of Physicians and Surgeons explains, 'On the scale of human awareness, hypnosis is at the opposite end from coma, with ordinary consciousness in the middle. Trance is an intensely focused and concentrated ribbon of attention that screens out external stimuli.

2. Hypnosis Is Not Being In Someone's Power

Despite the scientific consensus that hypnosis has come of age, many people still see it in terms of an active expert controlling a passive subject.

This idea of strong hypnotist vs weak subject dates back to Mesmer (hence 'mesmerize') in the eighteenth century, when hypnotism was strongly regarded as one of the devil's devices for gaining control of man's will. In fact, Mesmer was charged with using his arts to seduce women. The notion of the hypnotist as a dirty old man has lingered in the popular imagination.

The modern view, however, is far removed from these ancient ideologies.

Today many psychologists support the theory that the hypnotist acts merely as a guide to the hypnotic state – the subject performing the actual 'work' of transition.

3. *Hypnotizability Is Not a Sign of Mental Weakness*
As Dr H. Spiegel argues, 'On the contrary, it is a mark of intelligence and the ability to concentrate'.

Conditions Hypnosis Can Help
As a rule of thumb, if your G.P. cannot find anything wrong with you, then, hypnosis can be expected to be successful, provided:

- You have made up your mind to get rid of your problem.
- You believe in hypnosis.
- You have reasonably good concentration and imagination.
- You are willing to faithfully stick to the programme the hypnotist has designed for you.

The application of hypnosis to the following conditions is well known: overeating, smoking, insomnia, anxiety, emotional problems, depression, lack of confidence and motivation, phobias, obsessive or compulsive behaviour, nail-biting, thumb-sucking, lack of concentration, stuttering, some forms of sexual problems and identity deterioration. This is not, of course, an exhaustive list.

Hypnosis and Self-hypnosis
If what is essential in hypnosis is the subject's willingness and ability to concentrate exclusively and intensely on the hypnotist's suggestions, it follows that the subject must be highly motivated and know what to do. If this is the case he should be able to hypnotize himself (self-hypnosis) as effectively as being hypnotized by someone else (hetero-hypnosis). That is to say, self-hypnosis should be as effective as hetero-hypnosis! (Or, to put the point bluntly, that hetero-hypnosis is in fact a guided self-hypnosis).

This corollary has been fully corroborated by recent investigations. For example, two Brigham Young University researchers (Lynn Johnson and David Weight) tried both hetero- and self-hypnosis on 48 college students over a two-day period. Half the subjects were hypnotized by someone else the first day while the other half were told to hypnotize themselves using a special instruction booklet. The second day the two groups swapped methods. On both days each group was given the twelve 'suggestions'.

The students then rated their own responses to each of the suggestions and their scores were used as indications of their degree of hypnotic susceptibility. After each session, the subjects answered a set list of questions on their hypnotic experience.

It was found that:

—— Neither type of induction was superior to the other in producing general hypnotic behaviour in inexperienced subjects.
—— The general features of the hypnotic experience and the resulting behaviour were similar under both procedures.

Similarly, Dr J. Ruch from Stanford University has experimented with 88 student volunteers. These volunteers were divided into three main groups and underwent different modes of hypnosis. It was found that:

—— The subjects were able to hypnotize themselves without prior exposure to hetero-hypnotic experience.
—— Previous exposure to hetero-hypnosis can significantly inhibit performance in self-hypnosis.
—— Self-hypnosis can significantly enhance later hetero-hypnosis.

If self-hypnosis is as good as hetero-hypnosis, why, it may be asked, have only a very few people tried it? None of the subjects mentioned in the two studies cited here, for example, had ever attempted self-hypnosis prior to the experiments.

Dr Ruch suggests that this is the result of convention. We are too accustomed to the thought that true hypnosis without a hypnotist's intervention is a logical impossibility. As he put it,

Subject-reports after the study was over indicated a mixture of expectations, partly that they would not be successful at self-hypnosis without extensive training (the lay version of the conventional lore) and partly that if they were somehow to be successful they would then lose control (the lay version of hypnosis as a passive dissociated state, without self-direction or control).

The True Nature of Hypnosis

To summarize and elaborate briefly on what has been said so far. Firstly, hetero-hypnosis is no more than a guided self-hypnosis. When a hypnotist hypnotizes his patient, what in fact happens is that the patient hypnotizes himself, through the guidance of the hypnotist. This point has been corroborated by modern studies − that self-hypnosis is as effective as hetero-hypnosis. To put the point bluntly, there is no need (in principle) to see a hypnotist. You can do the job equally well by yourself (assuming, of course, that you have the knowledge and the motivation).

Secondly, hypnotic states and hypnotic phenomena are not mysterious, extraordinary states which are divorced from the reality of everyday life. We have all been under hypnotic state (and experienced hypnotic phenomena) when we are deeply absorbed in something. In fact, what a hypnotist does in his clinic is simply to extend and make more systematic use of this capacity. Needless to say, this is also the major aim of this book − to show the readers how they can develop and make more efficient use of their hypnotic capacity.

The understanding of this point should dispel, for once and for all, the notion that hypnosis is wicked. Nothing could be further from the truth. Hypnosis is good because it is the embodiment of the true potential of man. The realization of this point, I believe, has led to the now almost universal acceptance of hypnosis in the world of modern medicine.

Since the essence of hypnosis is the concentration of the subject, every change endeavour (relaxation therapy, sexual therapy, social skill training, etc.) is hypnotic in nature, as every change endeavour requires a certain amount of concentration on the part of the subject. No psychological strategy can work without this.

Yet, the fact remains that by using non-hypnotic psychological strategies in the explicit context of (self) hypnosis, their therapeutic effectiveness can be greatly enhanced. For example, Dr Lazarus has reported that 'Clients who requested hypnosis and received a standard relaxation sequence that substituted the word 'hypnosis' for 'relaxation' wherever possible, showed more subjective and objective improvements than those who received ordinary relaxation therapy.' Similarly, I have shown the beneficial effects of such an integration in the various journals.

A Model for the Effective Use of Self-hypnosis

There is no need to get bogged down here in the technical details. Suffice to say that all psychological strategies can be used in the explicit context of self-hypnosis, using the following model for the effective use of self-hypnosis which can be stated in terms of four basic steps.

Step 1: Making Concrete Formulation of Goal.

Step 2: Gaining Access to the Unconscious by means of Hypnotic state, Hypnotic trance, Hypnotic Relaxation.

Step 3: Self-suggestion (Positive Thinking) and/or Success Visualization.

Step 4: The 'As If' Principle and/or 'in Real Life' Activity (i.e. behaving as if the visualization were true).

Each one of the four steps can be used independently, and will still produce results. (Needless to say, the same can be said with regard to psychological strategies). Whenever possible, however, they have to be used as a whole, step by step, as this will produce the maximum result. For example, it is conventional to use Step 3 after Step 2 has been accomplished, as this will increase the therapeutic effectiveness of Step 3. There are, of course, exceptions. As you go through Chapters 4-16, you will see that, in some instances, only some of the steps are appropriate. For easy understanding, however, I will always try to make the appropriate steps explicit.

Each one of the four steps has an unlimited number of variations. In Chapters 4-16, several of these variations will be given – an attempt will be made to show how to use various psychological strategies with self-hypnosis techniques, and therefore to maximize their effects in dealing with specific problems.

As has been mentioned in the *Preface*, the first concrete use of the model will be described in Chapter 3 on Master Your Habits. In the chapters which follow, frequent reference will be made to Chapter 3. Thus, do make sure that you read and understand it thoroughly, even if you have no particular problem with your habits.

2.

What is Important in Hypnosis?

I have tried to emphasize that the hypnotic state is not a mysterious and extraordinary state. Each time we are deeply absorbed in something, we are in a form of hypnotic state.

This is not to say, of course, that there are no degrees of hypnotic state. As you continue to do it, you will be able to go deeper and deeper. The yardstick for measuring the degree of depth is the difference between the way you feel when you are under hypnosis and the way you feel prior to it. The more significant the change (the more relaxed, peaceful, etc. you feel) the deeper is your hypnotic state.

Basic Principles for Subjects

Someone who encounters hypnosis for the first time, however, tends to place unwarranted emphasis on this difference. Such a person typically tries to put himself under hypnotic state (or asks a hypnotist to do it) and upon realizing that the hypnotic state is not much different from the time he is deeply absorbed in something in daily life, concludes that he has not been hypnotized, and that hypnosis has not been effective.

This is unfortunate as, generally speaking, the depth of hypnosis bears no relationship to its therapeutic effectiveness. What is important in hypnosis is the subject's *willingness to perceive everything which happens as a manifestation of hypnotic state*. This is the first principle.

Sometime ago a man asked me to help him stop his drinking habit. In the first session, as usual, I took a complete life history and taught him a relaxation exercise (not self-hypnosis). I planned to do hypnosis in the second session. The patient, however, misunderstood the relaxation exercise for a complete hypnotic induction. Several days before the second session he rang me and said, 'I wish to cancel the appointment because I have stopped drinking. Thank's for hypnotizing me last week.'

Even though I had not hypnotized him, he thought that he had been hypnotized and therefore the relaxation exercise became hypnotic. This patient recovered because of the faith he had in hypnosis. He had an ability which is so crucial for the success of hypnosis – he *uncritically accepted everything the hypnotist did or said*. Martin Orne, a prominent hypnotist has called this attitude 'trance logic'.

Perhaps, it will clarify matters if I give four illustrations. They will also serve to illustrate another principle which is often even more important than the one already mentioned i.e. the subject's *willingness to carry out homework exercises* (Step 4 on the model for the effective use of self-hypnosis). Occasionally, this principle alone will do.

Case 1

A patient came to me for insomnia. After induction, she explicitly told me that I had not hypnotized her because she was aware of everything I said; but, at the same time, she suspected that she had been hypnotized. She faithfully carried out the homework and was able to sleep well after two weeks.

Case 2

A patient came to me for marijuana addiction and very heavy smoking. After induction, he told me that he had been in a deep hypnotic state. 'Why?' I asked. 'Because I felt slightly more relaxed', he replied. He faithfully carried out the homework and was able to cut his smoking rate from 30 to 0 and got rid of his addiction completely after just one week.

Case 3

A patient came to me for smoking. After induction, he told me that he experienced a dramatic change in his state of consciousness (i.e. felt so very relaxed, happy and calm) and subsequently concluded that he had been under a deep hypnotic state (and, indeed, he had been). At the second week, he cut his cigarette intake from 31 to 16. Afterwards, he found the homework too time-consuming and ceased doing it prematurely. He did not improve further.

Case 4

A patient came to me for overweight. After induction, she told me how different she felt. As I said 'deeper, deeper', she felt a very powerful force (like a whirlwind) pulling her deeper and deeper, and there was nothing she could do: In point of fact, she is highly hypnotizable and was in a deep state at that time. However, despite my explanation, she refused to believe that she had been hypnotized, as the experience is similar to her experience during Transcendental Meditation. She subsequently concluded that hypnosis was not appropriate. She never improved.

As hetero-hypnosis is nothing but a guided self-hypnosis, all I have said is directly applicable to those who wish to hypnotize themselves. Do your best at hypnotising yourself, and then confidently say, 'Yes, I have been under hypnotic state. I need no proof whatever'. Faithfully follow Step 4 on the model for the effective use of self-hypnosis (and you will find abundant examples of its use in Chapters 3-15). It is quite often indispensable, and it alone may do.

The Wrong Approach

There are several personal qualities which can prevent you from making rapid progress: *impatience* (lack of perseverance); *extreme practicality* (in the sense of disliking theoretical explanations); and *laziness* (in the sense of expecting magic). Let me illustrate what I mean by means of two cases.

Case 1

A lady came to me complaining of constant sense of tension. She had been to a medical hypnotherapist for three hourly sessions without any result whatever. Upon examination, it became clear that she did not get anything out of the sessions because during the attempted inductions she impatiently forced herself to enter a hypnotic state and analysed everything that was going on. Once this was understood, and once she was willing to patiently let go and not worry about the depth of the state, she was able to experience the sense of calmness and relaxation in half an hour only.

Case 2

An overweight lady came to me complaining of her uncontrollable eating habit. A standard procedure was carried out in the first session. At the second session, she said, 'I didn't get anything out of last weeks session. Nothing appears to have changed.' Upon examination, it became clear that she did not get anything out of the first session because she had been passively waiting for a magical transformation to occur, without any or very little effort on her part. It was explained that hypnosis is an active psychic activity, and that what she should have done was to actively do her homework, rather than passively waiting for something to happen to her. She understood and accepted this explanation. At the second session, she reported that she had been able to control her eating habit (even though she had to try hard). At the third session, she said, 'Fantastic, things appear to be happening automatically. I have not felt any compulsion to overeat at all.'

Let's go over what I have said. Firstly, the hypnotic state is a paradoxical state, as the more you worry about it, the more shallow it will be. So remember, the more patience you have, the deeper you will go. Secondly, the sincere acceptance of a theoretical explanation can have an immediate therapeutic and liberating effect. Thirdly, contrary to popular opinion, hypnosis is the greatest activity there is. The seemingly miraculous achievement is the side effect of high level concentrated activity.

You Can If You Think You Can

According to Perls,

> As long as you fight a symptom, it will become worse. If you take responsibility for what you are doing to yourself, how you produce your symptoms, how you produce your illness, how you produce your existence – the very moment you get in touch with yourself – growth begins, integration begins.

The great psychologist William James used to suffer from an overpowering nervous breakdown and despondency. His release was marked by a passage in his notebook dated 30 April, 1870.

> I think that yesterday was a crisis in my life. I finished the first part of Renouvier's second 'Essais' and see no reason why his

definition of Free Will – 'the sustaining of a thought because I choose to when I might have other thoughts' – need be the definition of an illusion. My first act of free will shall be to believe in free will.

That faith, that assumption which saved his life, he never abandoned. The belief in free will has a pragmatic value. The very moment you are convinced that you are a responsible free agent, a real progress starts to take place and growth begins. In fact, there is evidence that determinism (the belief that one is helpless and is completely at the mercy of the circumstances) more accurately describes the experience of the neurotic and the psychotic, and that free will (the belief that one is able, to a certain extent, to genuinely direct or choose one's own destiny) more adequately describes the experience of the healthy man.

It is now time to conclude this chapter with a brief summary. Firstly, do not ask, 'What is the proof that I have been hypnotized?' Rather, learn to perceive everything which happens in your attempt as a manifestation of hypnotic state. Also, when you are trying to enter an hypnotic state, it is not a good idea to intellectually analyse what is going on. Instead, gently but persistently let yourself go, in body and in mind. Thirdly, make sure that you have read Chapter 1 and this, chapter carefully and have understood them. Remember, the correct understanding of hypnosis is essential to its success. Lastly, do not wait for a magical transformation to occur, but, instead, faithfully carry out the 'in real life' exercises (Step 4 in the model) given in Chapters 3-15. This is indeed free will in activity. If you accept the above recommendations, then your progress is sure to be rapid.

3.

Master Your Habits

As has been mentioned in Chapter 1, this is a very important chapter as here, for the first time in this book, the application of the model for the effective use of self-hypnosis will be concretely described. Your benefiting fully from Chapters 4-15, depends on your correct understanding of this chapter. Thus, make sure that you do read and understand it thoroughly.

A large number of habits are counterproductive in nature. For example, it is probably wise to rid oneself of the following habits: perfectionism; smoking habit; worry habit; laziness; alcoholism; nail-biting; thumb-sucking; tardiness; sloppiness and the like.

I am sure you will agree that, on the other hand, the following habits are wholesome: cheerfulness; punctuality; compassion; self-discipline; charity; self-respect; the habit of dressing neatly.

Human beings are, according to an old saying, 'creatures of habit'. Your habits govern your life and you need them to function in the world. For example, upon waking up on a weekday morning you habitually brush your teeth, wash yourself, put on your clothes, and eat some kind of breakfast. If you had not developed these and other socially acceptable habits, you would not be tolerated in your community.

It is therefore a good idea to break bad habits and strengthen desirable habits.

Changing one's habit is not, however, an easy endeavour. As Mark Twain remarked, 'It is easy to quit smoking. I have done it a dozen times'.

In order to be able to master your habits and control your destiny, you need to be able to answer the following questions affirmatively.

1. Do you believe that you can change your habits?

2. Are you willing to put in a substantial amount of effort and energy to direct yourself toward positive habit patterns that will make your life more rewarding?

Step 1: Making Concrete Formulation of Goal

It is obvious that some goals are, in principle, abstract (e.g. I want to increase my general sense of well-being). Whenever possible, however, always specify your goal in such a way so that it has three characteristics:

1. It is specific (measurable = countable)
2. It is positive
3. It locates the goal within some environment or situation

Thus:
- *Instead of saying:*
  I would like to be more assertive (too abstract and is not located within some environment or situation).
  Say:
  I would like to be able to say 'no' to requests which are unreasonable at home.
- *Instead of saying:*
  I wish I were a better person.
  Say:
  I would like to be able to keep control of my staff and gain their respect.
- *Instead of saying:*
  I would like to be more successful in life.
  Say:
  I would like to be able to earn more money during my spare time.
- *Instead of saying:*
  I wish I wasn't so stupid when it comes to remembering things – (too negative and is not located within some environment or situation).
  Say:
  I would like to be able to remember facts and figures and recall them quickly in a discussion.

Each time you behave in the way you want to avoid, make note of it. Pay special attention to the various situations under which it occurs and its consequences. At night, before going to bed, sum them up. Carry this out for one week before attempting to change your behaviour through self-hypnosis and chart the results. This will provide you with an accurate assessment of your condition. You may end up with something like this.

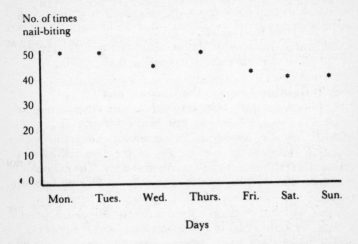

Days

The recording procedure needs to be carried out before, during and after the treatment programme. Its function is threefold. Firstly, it will provide you with an objective indication of your progress. Secondly, it will serve as a source of reinforcement. That is to say, as you see the chart bending in the desired direction, you will feel good and want to persist to the end. And thirdly, it will help you to become a better observer of your own behaviour and the factors that influence it, including your thoughts as well as environmental factors, so that you will be able to exert more influence over your behaviour and achieve more success in attaining your goal. 'In several research studies', says Drs Rathus and Nevid,[1] 'the act of self-recording alone has led to changes in the rate of occurrence of the problem behaviour. ... people who merely kept records of their smoking frequency wound up decreasing their smoking rate.'

Occasionally, it is necessary to break the end goal into the preliminary component steps (sub goals) and set weekly goals for yourself to master each of the targeted habits gradually. For example, the end goal 'meeting a man who is interested in more than a brief affair' usually necessitates several sub-goals.

Sub Goal 1: Physical attractiveness, achieved through proper beauty care, attractive clothing and weight reduction.

Sub Goal 2: Adequate personal resources, achieved through reading current news magazines and attending adult classes.

Sub Goal 3: Interpersonal skill, achieved through learning to behave more assertively and appropriately.

Step 2: Gaining Access to the Unconscious

Use either a naturally occurring period when the unconscious is most accessible (such as just before retiring at night or immediately after awakening in the morning) or create such a situation through the use of one of the two self-hypnotic relaxation techniques to be described shortly. The rationale of this procedure can be described as follows. During hypnotic trance, suggestions work far more powerfully because we are relaxed, with our physical senses in relative abeyance. In such a state, we gain access to the unconscious and not only do we accept suggestions from someone else more readily, we also accept our own suggestions more easily.

Technique 1

Imagine, as vividly as possible, a place where you feel good, relaxed and at peace for a few minutes and allow the relaxation, warmness and heaviness to grow. (It might be a mountainside, a beach, a friend's bedroom, wherever you have actually experienced relaxation and calmness.) Gradually, instruct each part of your body to let go, becoming loose and limp. Then, relax with whatever image comes up for you. Stay with this for another three to five minutes.

Technique 2

Be attentive to your breathing for one minute. Then begin to be aware of the different parts of your body – feet, legs, pelvis, stomach, chest, back, shoulders, neck, face, head and scalp – seeing each part from the inside and noticing how tense or relaxed it feels.

Now go back to any body part that felt tense one by one. Each time you breathe out, imagine that your body tension and energy are fading away, drifting away from these parts of your body one at a time. Notice how the tightness and tension are released little by little, effortlessly.

When you have done this with each part of your body that felt tense, bring your attention back to your breath and enjoy the changed quality of body sensation.

Generally speaking, after Step 2 has been completed, you should proceed to Step 3, but, it should be mentioned that, in some instances, Step 2 is adequate on its own. Disappearance of symptoms frequently occurs in the hypnotic state without any specific curative suggestion being made. As Dr Kuriyama[2] reports, '… in many cases mere induction into hypnosis can bring out marked improvement or more or less disappearance of symptoms without any therapeutic suggestions or interpretations being given. Often simply being in a trance seems to be very therapeutic.'

Step 3: Self-suggestion (Positive Thinking) and/or Success Visualization

Suggest to yourself the things you want. In so doing, pay attention to the following two rules.

Rule 1

The suggestion has to be uttered with understanding, faith, and full appreciation of its relevance and profundity. It has to be felt to be true. As Jesus Christ said, 'If thou canst believe – all things are possible to him that believeth' (Mark 9:23), and 'According to your faith be it unto you' (Matthew 9:29).

Rule 2

The suggestion has to be repeated three times at a given time, several times per day. As Mandino (the author of *The Greatest Salesman in the World*) put it,

> Herein lies the hidden secret of all man's accomplishments. As I repeat the words daily they will soon become a part of my active mind, but more important, they will also seep into my other mind, that mysterious source which never sleeps, which creates my dreams, and often makes me act in ways I do not comprehend.

The suggestion has to be reasonable and must sound right

to you. This is what Weatherhead caught sight of when he wrote,

> Behind all the discoveries of psychologists since Mesmer ... lies one of the great truths about the mind. It may be expressed as follows: if the mind really accepts an idea as true, and if the idea is *reasonable*, it tends, by means of unconscious processes, to actualize itself or come true. To bring about the entry of an integrating idea into the mind, so that the idea may 'come true' is called treatment by suggestion.

Similarly, Emile Coué, the father of 'auto-suggestion' has argued that whatever thought we continually hold in our minds, provided it is reasonable, tends to become an actual condition of our life.

Also, the suggestion has to be brief, simple and clear. This, however, does not mean that the suggestion has to be direct (i.e. of the form 'I will do such and such'.) Indirect suggestion, as Milton H. Erickson has proven, can often circumvent resistance and penetrate the subconscious mind much more easily and deeply. This is especially true when the suggestion is constituted by 'famous quotations', since they often emit a sense of reason and radiate the atmosphere of 'certainty' and 'universality'.

Let me now give you a few examples.

Direct Suggestion
—— General well-being:
   Day by day, in every way, I am getting better and better (Coué).
—— Calmness:
   Every day, I shall be calm and confident, relaxed and happy, even when there is no reason for being so.
—— Smoking:
   Day by day, it will be easier and easier for me to say no to a cigarette.
—— Overeating:
   Day by day, it will be easier and easier for me to say 'no' to fattening food. With each passing day, I shall enjoy physical activity more and more.
—— Inner peace:
   I totally forgive anyone who needs my forgiveness, both now and in the past; I fully and completely

forgive. I am totally forgiven by anyone who needs to forgive me, both now and in the past; I am fully and completely forgiven.

Indirect Suggestion
—— Guilt (Excessive):
Guilt is the greatest waste of emotional energy since no amount of guilt can ever change history. My feeling guilty will not change the past, nor will it make me a better person. Guilt prevents me from using the here and now in any kind of effective, self-enhancing way. I am not going to use guilt to transfer responsibility for my behaviour from myself to others. Guilt is not the healthy way to get something.
—— Worry (Excessive):
Not one moment of worry will make things any better. In fact, worry will very likely help me to be less effective in dealing with the present. I am determined to banish this neurotic behaviour from my life.
—— Anger (Excessive):
Anger serves no utilitarian purpose. It has nothing to do with being a happy, fulfilled person. The world and the people in it do not have to succumb to my wish. Others have the right to be different from what I would prefer.
—— Self-discipline:
Put off until tomorrow only what you are willing to die having left undone. (Picasso).
—— Listening Skill:
He who hath knowledge spareth his words (Proverbs 17:27). Nature has given man one tongue, but two ears, that we may hear from others twice as much as we speak. (Epicetetus).
—— Stress Management Principle:
If you are distressed by anything external, the pain is not due to the thing itself but to your estimate of it. This, you have the power to revoke at any time. (M. Aurelius).
—— Accepting Others As They Are:
If I keep from meddling with people,
They will take care of themselves.
If I keep from commanding people,

They will behave themselves,
If I keep from preaching at people,
They will improve themselves,
If I keep from improving on people,
They become themselves. (Lao tze)
—— Love:
Lord, make me an instrument of your peace
Where there is hatred, let me sow love.
Where there is injury, pardon.
Where there is doubt, faith.
Where there is despair, hope.
Where there is darkness, light.
Where there is sadness, joy.
O Divine Master, grant that I may not so much seek
To be consoled, as to console,
To be understood, as to understand,
To be loved, as to love,
For; It is in giving that we receive. It is in pardoning,
that we are pardoned. It is in dying that we are born
to eternal life (St Francis of Assisi).

Success Visualization
Another strategy you can apply during Step 3 is 'success
visualization'. It operates as follows. Build up a very vivid
picture of yourself behaving in the way you want to behave,
being the sort of person you want to be, and letting this image
drift into your mind on the occasions decided upon in Step 1.
Continue for ten minutes. Dr Stanton has commented on this
procedure.

> Perhaps the greatest power we have as human beings is to use our
> imagination to help us change in the ways we want to change. We
> are often exhorted to use our will power to effect change but most
> people find this does not help them to any great extent, and,
> unfortunately, feel very guilty about their weakness. It seems far
> easier, and much more effective to use imagination to help us
> change. The way to do this would appear to be to create in one's
> mind an image of the person one wants to be. The value of this
> approach ... has been repeatedly affirmed in my own therapy
> practice.

Next, wake yourself up by means of the following
procedure: "In a moment, I am going to wake myself up. I am

going to count from one to three. On the count of three, I shall be completely and totally wide awake, refreshed and feeling absolutely tremendous. 'One'. I can feel the normal body tone creeping back into my arms and legs. 'Two'. Normal muscle tensions creeping through my entire body, as I come up closer and closer to the surface. Almost there now, almost there. 'Three'. I am wide awake, refreshed and feeling so absolutely relaxed.''

And finally, should you wish, you can put Step 2 and 3 onto tape and play it whenever the need arises. If you decide to do this, make sure you allow ample 'pause' after Step 2 has been completed, to allow 'hypnotic relaxation' to develop fully.

Step 4: The 'As If' Principle and/or Real Life Activity
Strengthen the effect of Step 3 by acting as if it has come true. Conduct yourself as if you were who you want to be. As Shakespeare said, 'Assume a virtue if you have it not.' This strategy is called the 'as if' principle, and a complete description of it will be given in Chapter 14.

Additionally, the 'as if' principle can be coupled with real life activity. I would like to suggest two for this particular chapter.

How To Keep Your Spirits High
Knowing what to do intellectually is sometimes not enough. The spirit may be willing, but unfortunately, more often than not, the flesh is weak. If you are in this position, try the following tips.

Firstly, enlist your family's help. Post your chart in the most strategic places in the house and have your family convey approval for your progress and disapproval (although with implied encouragement) for not meeting your goal. That is, have them say, 'We are disappointed with what you did this week and we hope that you will do better next week. We know you can.' This strategy makes use of the 'losing face' principle. Since you have made the announcement, you feel compelled to continue, or else you lose face. This, in turn, could only help to make the task easier and you have the moral support of your family.

Secondly, reward yourself at the end of each week with a pre-planned gift if you have met your weekly goal. The reward must be highly pleasurable (e.g. money, small gift, favoured activity, etc).

Lastly, examine your note to determine the factors that maintain the habit you wish to change and manipulate them in a way which is conducive to your goal. For example, if you are poor at studying and find that the usual consequence of leaving your book is that you switch on the television, reverse the situation and make television viewing contingent on studying a certain amount of time. That is to say, allow yourself to watch television only after you have spent a certain amount of time studying.

Taking Control of Your Environment

Granting that (a) you know exactly what to do and (b) you are highly motivated, you may still find it difficult to change the old habit due to the influence of certain stimulus conditions. It is therefore necessary to subdue your 'world' (the environment you come into contact with).

Firstly, if the bad habit occurs frequently in a variety of places, restrict it to one environment only. For example, if you feel that you must suck your thumb while watching the television news, remove yourself to your thumb-sucking area (e.g. bathroom).

The function of this strategy is threefold. (1) It weakens the association between the bad habit and the various stimulus conditions, thereby reducing the likelihood of that behaviour recurring. (2) You are forced to put off the behaviour, which may permanently interrupt your otherwise automatic habit. (3) If the area you have chosen is particularly unpleasant, this will heighten the cost of repeating the habit.

Secondly, review your note to determine whether it is feasible to change your stimulus *milieu* to alter the frequency of the problem behaviour. For example, if you have a problem losing weight because you routinely set yourself by the television with boxes of crackers and potato chips, watch less television until you have developed a degree of mastery over your problem.

Thirdly, look again at your note and identify the connection between the stimulus condition and the bad habit (e.g. feeling lonely and overeating; sitting in a library lounge and daydreaming). Next, attempt to replace the old habit with a new, competing habit. The new habit must be incompatible with the old habit (e.g. replace 'smoking' with 'jogging'; 'overeating' with 'breathing exercises').

Finally, whenever possible, expose yourself to existing situations that lead to the life-enhancing habit patterns. For example, if you feel that you can study better in the library, then make use of the library more often.

As you carry out the tips given here, the old habit will gradually dwindle and be replaced by a new life-enhancing habit. In turn, this indicates that you have attained mastery over your habit and possessed the ability to control your destiny. As William James put it,

Sow an action and
You reap a habit;
Sow a habit and
You reap a character;
Sow a character and
You reap a destiny.

4.

Managing Fear and Anxiety

In this chapter, I want to mention two ways to manage fear and anxiety: a modified version of 'self control desensitization' and meditation.

Self-Control Desensitization

The most widely used technique to deal with anxiety or fear is 'systematic desensitization' (S.D.) During the application of this technique the patient (under a state of deep relaxation) is exposed to various anxiety-provoking stimuli, imaginatively, one at a time and at an increasing level of aversiveness. The patient is cured when he is able to experience the most aversive anxiety-inducing stimulus without adverse consequences.

S.D. is still the best method when the client presents himself with one simple phobia of clearly defined nature (e.g. cat phobia, urinal phobia, etc).

The trouble starts when the client has a lot of fears, or when his anxiety is free floating or not easily definable.

Professor Goldfried from State University of New York at Stoony Brook has reported that 'after relaxation training has begun, but prior to desensitization proper, clients frequently report, "The treatment is really working. I find myself becoming less anxious in a number of situations".'

This and similar observations have led Professor Goldfried to formulate a new approach to the management of fear and anxiety – Self-control Desensitization. This approach stresses the use of relaxation as an active coping skill to soothe away tension in a variety of anxiety-inducing situations. That is to say, it aims to train the client to become more sensitive to the sensations of tension (regardless of the external situation eliciting it) and eventually to use these sensations of tension as a signal for voluntary relaxation. In this regard 'one has', says Professor Goldfried, 'an effective self-control procedure that can generalize, both over situations and time'.

Step 1: Making Concrete Formulation of Goal

See Chapter 3. It has to be admitted, however, that it is not very easy in this situation to follow precisely the tips given there. You may just wish to say, I want to be able to relax in such and such a situation (e.g. public speaking situation, when driving a car, when faced with a barking dog, etc).

Step 2: Gaining Access to the Unconscious

Use the procedure taught in Chapter 3 to put yourself into hypnotic state. Then, carry out the following steps:

Step 1

Experience fully whatever is happening inside you in the here and now. Let happen whatever is happening for ten minutes.

This procedure will eventually enable you to gradually detach yourself from yourself and to deal with the unacceptable parts of your being in a more constructive fashion. As Drs Beahrs and Humiston put it, 'In emotional illness, it is not the feelings in themselves which constitute the problem; it is the struggle at trying to fight them off.'

Essentially, the same point has been made by Carl Rogers, a famous psychologist.

> The dilemma of our unhappiness lies within us. Our irritability, our nagging, our whining, and all the other ways our negative emotions are channelled – all these prevent us from owning our emotions. The key to resolving the dilemma of emotions is simply to own them – that is, to own up to the fact that these emotions and behaviour are ours, that we are creating them, and that all the blaming in the world will help us not one iota. The only way to get over whining, nagging and jealousy is to own up to them and then decide to work on ourselves to change ourselves – not others.

Step 2

Breathe easily and comfortably for five minutes. Gradually, deepen your breathing without forcing yourself. Each time you breathe out, say, 'calm' and feel yourself letting go of the tensions, unwinding, feeling the calmness and relaxation flowing all through your mind and body.

With diligent practice, you will have more and more control over your mind. As a Buddhist meditation master once wrote, 'Keeping the mind under control is like tethering a wild bull. He calms down after a while. Finally, he becomes so used to the tether that even if you release him he will not go away.'

Step 3

Breathe deeply. Hold your breath and experience fully the tensed sensation of holding one's breath. When you can no longer hold it, let it go, say 'calm' and feel yourself letting go of the tensions, unwinding, feeling the calmness and relaxation flowing all through your mind and body. Repeat five times.

Step 4

Make a light fist with your right hand and give your exclusive attention to it. Say, 'TENSE'; tense it completely and study the sensation fully. Say, 'RELAX'; relax it completely and study carefully the consequent sensation. Repeat the procedure with the left hand, the left leg, the right leg, the stomach, the chest and shoulders, the lips, the eyelids and neck.

Step 5

Combine Step 3 and Step 4 above. Breathe deeply and make a light fist with your right hand. Hold your breath, tense it completely and study the sensation (resulting from holding one's breath and tensing one's fist) fully. When you can no longer hold your breath, let it go, say, 'CALM' and feel yourself letting go of the tensions, unwinding, feeling the calmness and relaxation flowing all through your mind and body. Repeat with other regions.

Carry out steps 1-5 for one week. Their function is twofold. Firstly, they train you to become aware of your inner processes, with specific emphasis on the identification of the sensations of 'inner tension'. Secondly, they teach you to use 'breathing out' and self-command, 'CALM' as a cue for inducing calmness and tranquillity.

Step 3: Self-suggestion (Positive Thinking) and/or Success Visualization

Imagine, as vividly as possible an anxiety-evoking situation. Be aware of the sensation of 'inner tension' which emerges and experience it fully for ten seconds. Take a deep breath and as you let it go, say 'CALM' and feel yourself letting go of the tensions, unwinding, feeling the calmness and relaxation flowing all through your mind and body. If the anxiety has not sufficiently dissipated, stay in the imagined situation and repeat the procedure a few times. Should this attempt fail too, start with a less aversive situation and gradually work toward the most aversive.

Occasionally, it is wise to combine this approach with the use of 'rational' statements.

After reviewing relevant studies, Professor Goldfried concludes that the use of 'rational' statements is especially effective in cases of pervasive anxiety, or instances where the anxiety is mediated by concerns regarding the evaluation of others.

In using this combination, mentally shout the 'rational' statement when letting go of your breath (instead of using the self-command, 'CALM').

Everyone has to find out for himself the rational statement which sounds right for him. The following suggestions, therefore, must be seen strictly as such.

—— Misfortune:
   It is not the end of the world.
—— Public Speaking Phobia:
   It would be nice if the audience likes my speech.
—— Inferiority Complex:
   I am a valuable worthwhile person because I am a human being.
—— Interpersonal Anxiety:
   I have the right to be popular. I have the right to speak up. I have the right to make mistakes.
—— Stuttering:
   Bastard, you owe me respect and honour.
—— Exam fear:
   The more I worry, the worse will be my performance.
—— Sexual fear:

There is nothing either good or bad, but thinking makes it so. ETC.

Step 4: Real Life Activity

Go out to the real world and relax away, by means of the procedure taught here, any sensation of 'inner tension' which accrues during your daily life. Do not be discouraged if some initial difficulties are encountered. Relaxation is a complicated skill and requires a certain amount of practice before it can be effectively employed. As Jung put it, 'Consciousness is not achieved without pain'.

Each time you succeed in relaxing away your anxiety in real life, vividly imagine important people in your life patting you on the back and telling you how they admire your self-control. Smile, and allow yourself to bask in the warmth generated by your accomplishment. Tell yourself how much better off you are than people who have not yet learned to master the bodily sensations of anxiety.

EPILOGUE:

As a form of mental training (meditation), self-control desensitization is similar to Ainslie Meares 'Mental Ataraxis' which proceeds from an attempt to induce calmness in a comfortable position (e.g. sitting down in a deep chair) to an attempt to maintain the calmness obtained in the situations of discomfort (e.g. in the middle of an argument). As the ancients said, 'Meditation in activity is a hundred, a thousand, a million times superior to meditation in repose.'

As one persistently practises self-control desensitization, relaxing away anxiety will gradually be transformed into a 'habit'. That is to say, the time will come when a sensation of 'inner tension' will be automatically followed by a 'relaxation' response. The following case was reported by Drs Rathus and Nevid.

A twenty-two-year-old graduate student in educational psychology experienced anxiety in which shortness of breath was predominant. Diligent practice resulted in her *automatically* taking and releasing a deep breath in stressful situations, typically, confrontations with a passive father and demanding stepmother. Her exhaling was followed by deep, regular breathing and a quelling of other components of anxiety.

Remember that the above case only utilized a normal relaxation procedure. By putting it in the context of self-hypnosis as we are doing here, we should get a better outcome.

5.

The Power of Meditation

Meditation is a form of self-hypnosis, but, of a very unusual sort. It is supposed to generate a variety of non-specific beneficial effects, and it is not easy to make all of them concrete. For this reason as well, there is no Step 3 (self-suggestion) or Step 4 ('in real life' activity) in meditation. Of the four steps for the effective use of self-hypnosis, only Step 2 (gaining access to the unconscious) is appropriate. In this context, this step is equivalent to the instruction of how to meditate. As you go through this chapter, it is useful to bear in mind that meditation is essentially *the great art of letting go*.

How to Meditate

1. Sit quietly in a comfortable position with your eyes closed in a cosy, quiet and dimly-lit room. If possible, use the 'lotus' posture. Otherwise, practise in a straight-backed chair.
2. Deeply relax all your muscles, beginning at your feet and progressing up to your face. Keep them deeply relaxed.
3. Choose either one of the following three methods.

Method A
Breathe through your nose. Become aware of your breathing. As you breathe in, say the word 'in' and as you breath out, say the word 'calm' silently to yourself.

A variation of this method is found in the *Philokalia*, a compendium of the writings of Greek fathers and the masters of Byzantine spirituality.

> You know, brother, how we breathe, we breathe the air in and out. On this is based the life of the body and on this depends its warmth. So, sitting down in your cell, collect your mind, lead it along the path of the breath, along which the air enters in, constrain it to enter the heart altogether with inhaled air, and keep it there. Keep it there, but do not leave it silent and idle,

instead give it the following prayer: 'Lord, Jesus Christ, Son of God, have mercy upon me'. Let this be its constant occupation, never to be abandoned. For this work, by keeping the mind free from dreaming, renders it unassailable to suggestions of the enemy and leads it to Divine desire and love.

Method B

Pick up a word which you feel will help you to relax and conserve your energy (e.g. OM, MU, etc). Repeat it slowly and silently over and over again. The author of *The Cloud of Unknowing* has described this method.

Choose whatever one you prefer, or if you like, choose another that suits your tastes, provided that it is of one syllable. And clasp this word tightly in your heart so that it never leaves it, no matter what may happen. This word shall be your shield and your spear whether you ride in peace or in war. With this word you shall beat upon the cloud and the darkness, which are above you. With this word you shall strike down thoughts of every kind and drive them beneath the cloud of forgetting.

Method C

Stop thinking, quiet your mind, forget your existence and feel yourself sinking into a point just below the navel (the Japanese call it 'tanden' or 'kikai' which, roughly, means 'the sea of energy'). This method is beautifully expressed by Chuang Tzu.

Yen Hui said, 'I have made some progress.'

'What do you mean?' asked Confucius.

'I have forgotten humanity and righteousness', replied Yen Hui.

'Very good, but that is not enough', said Confucius.

On another day Yen Hui saw Confucius again and said, 'I have made some progress.'

'What do you mean?' asked Confucius.

'I have forgotten ceremonies and music', replied Yen Hui.

'Very good, but that is not enough', said Confucius.

Another day Yen Hui saw Confucius again and said, 'I have made some progress.'

'What do you mean?' asked Confucius.

Yen Hui said, 'I forget everything while sitting down.'

Confucius' face turned pale. He said, 'What do you mean by sitting down and forgetting everything?'

'I cast aside my limbs', replied Yen Hui, 'discard my intelligence, detach from both body and mind, and become one with the Great Universal (Tao). This is called sitting down and forgetting everything.'

Confucius said, 'When you become one with the Great Universal, you will have no partiality, and when you are part of the process of transformation, you will have no constancy. You are really a worthy man.

A modified version of this method, for the specific aim of developing *inner peace (calmness)* has been described by Jencks.

Permit yourself to go, during exhalations, to your centre, your centre of gravity, the middle of your body. Imagine going down into it in an elevator, climbing down a ladder, sliding down a rope, or any other way that appeals to you. Exhale and go down along the guide rope of the exhalation. Go down and down, stepwise or in one swoop, to the lowest place where you can imagine the centre to be. For most, this is somewhere below the level of the navel.

And there, in the centre, make room during exhalation. Create your place of privacy, a place all your own, within yourself; a place to go, to turn to, whenever and wherever you need it. Have there what you need. Remove from it all that is useless or disturbing. Allow in, or exclude, anybody you wish. Be with others or alone.

If your outside world seems too big, too exhausting, too confusing, make the inner world cosy and comfortable, small, simple, safe, secure, secluded, and still. If your outside world is too small, too restricted, and restricting, too depressed and depressing, too dark and dreary, make the inner world wide, and open and expanded, elaborate and elegant, light and bright, elating and inspiring.

Professor Herbert Benson from Harvard Medical School has argued that no technique of meditation can claim uniqueness.

There is not a single method that is unique in eliciting the Relaxation Response. For example, T.M. is one of the many techniques that incorporate these components.* However, we believe it is not necessary to use the specific method and specific secret, personal sound taught by T.M. Tests at the Thorndike Memorial Laboratory at Harvard have shown that a similar

---

* Steps 1-6 mentioned here.

technique used with any sound or phrase or prayer or mantra brings forth the same physiological changes noted during T.M. – decreased oxygen consumption, decreased carbon-dioxide elimination, decreased rate of breathing. In other words, using the basic necessary components, *any one of the age-old or the newly derived techniques produces the same physiological results regardless of the mental device used*.

4. Continue for 20 minutes. Occasionally, open your eyes to check the time. When you finish, sit quietly for several minutes at first with closed eyes and later with open eyes.

5. Do not worry about whether you are successfully achieving a deep level of relaxation. Let yourself go completely and allow relaxation to occur at its own pace. When distracting thoughts or interruptions (e.g. telephone ringing) occur, gently ignore them and return to the task as conveniently as possible. Your mind should at all time be clear and still. With practice, the response should come with little effort.

This attitude is called 'passive detachment', and according to Professor Benson it is the *most important element in meditation*. It can be epitomized by the following story, given to us by Alan Watts.

A story is told of a man who came to Buddha with offerings of flowers in both hands. The Buddha said, 'Drop it!' So he dropped the flowers in his left hand. The Buddha said again, 'Drop it!' He dropped the flowers in his right hand. And the Buddha said, 'Drop that which you have neither in the right nor in the left, but in the middle!' And the man was instantly enlightened.

Similarly; Ashvagosha, an eminent Buddhist of the first century A.D. formulated the attitude in this way.

As to the practice of checking vain thoughts, it should be done in a quiet place, properly seated and in a proper spirit ... for all kinds of ideas, as soon as thought of, must be put away, even the idea of banishing them must also be put away. As all existence originally came to be without any idea of its own, it ceases to be also without any idea of its own; any thoughts arising therefore must be from being absolutely passive. Nor must one follow the mind in its excursions to everything outside itself and then chase that thought away. If the mind wanders far away, it must be brought back into its proper state. One should know that the proper state is that of the soul alone without anything outside of it.

6. Practise the technique twice daily and not within two hours after any meal, since digestion, making the body more active, seems to interfere with the process of relaxation.

Comprehensive Psychological Integration

During the practice of meditation, it is usual to experience a number of thoughts, feelings and images which tend to compete with the task in hand. Many of these ideas have an affective or emotional value. This fact has been noted by Drs Gluck and Stroebel.

> The weakening of the repression barrier that occurs in sleep and in other altered states of consciousness, such as free association during the process of psychoanalytic therapy, may be produced in a relatively simple fashion during ... meditation. This would offer an explanation of a phenomenon that has been reported by a number of investigators, and which we have seen repeatedly in our patients. During meditation, thoughts and ideas may appear that are ordinarily repressed, such as intensely hostile or aggressive drives, murderous impulses, and occasionally, libidinal ideation.

As the fifth step indicates, the meditator is instructed to react with passive detachment to these thoughts and feelings, returning to the task as conveniently as possible. Since a wide variety of fear-related thoughts are reacted to in a relaxed and passive attitude, meditation serves as a strategy to cope with anxiety in general. It is a natural self-desensitization procedure.

Energy Building

The meditator's state of mind can be compared with a deep and dreamless sleep in which the mind is swept clean of all images and thoughts of subject-object relationship. The *Sutra* describes it like this!

> All that has its own characteristic or form ... is empty of the form: no arising, no ceasing; no contamination, no lack of contamination; no increase, no decrease. Therefore, in emptiness is no physical component, no sensation, no representation, no will, no consciousness; no eye, no ear, no nose, no tongue, no body, no mind; no shape, no colour, no sound, no smell, no taste, no touch, no concept; no visible world ... no consciously perceivable world; no ultimate ignorance, no extinction of

ultimate ignorance, no ageing and dying; no suffering, no cause of suffering, no extinction of suffering, no practice which leads to the extinction of suffering; no knowing, no attainment, no non-attainment.

In this state, the life force which is centred in the belly may easily rise up, giving great energy to the person who has mastered this great art of 'non-self' or 'mind'.

In his *The Inner Eye of Love* (Collins, 1978), William Johnston, Director of the Institute of Oriental Religions of Sophia University, writes,

> [The art] can be achieved without any faith whatever. It can be practised in a purely secular situation in order to develop human potential and ability to play ping pong or golf. It can be used for good or evil, to heal or to destroy, a grim fact which is well known in Japan.

On the medical side, the energy obtained, according to Dr Chen Yingning from Ping Feng Mountain Convalescent Hospital in Hang Chow, can cure

> ... all diseases related to mental and physical weakness such as dizziness, vertigo, tinnitus aurium, palpitation of the heart, timidity, insomnia, nightmares, impatience, fear, anger, sentimentality, emotional unsteadiness, amnesia, skinniness, poor digestion, lethargy, weariness, etc.

This of course assumes that the individual has no fundamental physical problems.

Centering
Alvin Toffler has popularized the term 'future shock' (*Future Shock*, Pan Books, 1973) to describe the disastrous effect of the accelerating pace of the modern world on human life. Too much change too fast causes deterioration of emotional and mental well-being. As he remarks,

> What remains? What is there of 'self' or 'personality' in the sense of a continuous, durable internal structure? For some, the answer is very little. For they are no longer dealing in 'self' but in what might be called 'serial selves'.

In order to cope with these rapid environmental changes, we need to have a strong sense of 'ego identity' which is defined by E. Erickson as,

... an awareness of the fact that there is a self-sameness and continuity to the ego's synthesizing methods, the style of one's individuality, and that this style coincides with the sameness and continuity of one's meaning for significant others in the immediate community.

Frederick Perls, a noted Gestalt therapist had explained the value of this inner stability further in his *Gestalt Therapy Verbatim* (Bantam Books, 1972).

If you are centred in yourself, then you don't adjust anymore ... then you assimilate, you understand, you are related to whatever happens ... Without a centre ... there is no place from which to work ... Achieving a centre, being grounded in oneself, is about the highest state a human can achieve.

By allowing the individual to regain his vital centre of energy, meaning and continuity, meditation becomes the necessary antidote to 'future shock'. By closing our eyes, gazing inward and returning to our 'self', we can experience this centre which lies at the core of our being.

Dr H.H. Bloomfield, Director of Psychiatry at the Institute of Psychophysiological Medicine in San Diego, California puts the point in the following way.

A centred individual can fully enjoy life. He is free from the continual need to adjust and modify himself to meet demands of his activity. Instead, he experiences an inner foundation from which he can fully assimilate, understand, and work with the world. This platform of inner stability provides a basis for consistent successful action and growing fulfilment.

6.

Losing Weight

The following statement, made in 1958 by a psychologist, Stunkard seems equally true today – 'Most obese patients will not remain in treatment. Of those who do remain in treatment, most will not lose significant poundage, and of those who do lose weight, most will regain it promptly.'

Most participants of weight-reduction programmes go on diets. But, after achieving their initial weight loss, gradually sneak back to their old eating habits. Before they know it, all their lost weight creeps back, plus more.

What are bad eating habits? If you answer the following questions affirmatively, it is certain that your eating habits are not good.

- Do you eat between meals?
- Do you eat while watching TV?
- Are you a social eater?
- Do you eat because others are eating?
- Do you eat quickly and finish everything on your plate?
- Are you unaware of your calorie intake?

The most important element in an effective weight reduction programme is a total reconstruction of your eating habits. Additionally, regular exercise will definitely help.

Step 1: Making Concrete Formulation of Goal
Apply the tips given in Chapter 3 with specific reference to the regulation of *calorie intake*. More specifically, weigh yourself and buy a calorie book. Then, each time you put something into your mouth, record its calorific value. At night, before you go to bed, jot down your intake of calories for the day. Carry this out for one week before attempting to reduce your weight and chart the results. Determine how many pounds you wish to shed altogether (e.g. 20 pounds), and how many pounds per week. As a rule of thumb, one pound per week is

leisurely; to aim at losing two pounds is ambitious. A key figure is this; each pound of weight equals 3,500 calories. Thus, if you want to lose one pound per week, you should reduce your intake of calories by 500 per day. Use your calorie book to plan meals and snacks within this calorie limit and to obtain proper nutrients. Whatever your calorie goal, plan your diet for the coming week beforehand in order to stay within those limits. As you make progress, the amount of calories ingested can be further reduced.

During the programme, your attention should be focused on reducing the intake of calories, and not on reducing your weight. The reason is this: As your intake of calories declines, your weight will automatically decline as well. This, in turn, will give you a 'push'. If, on the other hand, you concentrate on reducing your weight, as you see the slow progress (and it is a matter of plain fact that weight declines far more slowly than intake of calories), you may be discouraged and discontinue the effort.

Some subjects in Romanczyk's weight-control study monitored their daily body weight while other subjects monitored both their daily body weight and intake of calories. The result suggested that significant weight loss occurred only when calories were counted.

One thing is worth mentioning here, never reduce the intake of calories solely for its own sake. Rather, select low-calorie foods which you enjoy and prepare them to look attractive. Change your menu daily.

Apart from reducing your intake of calories directly, physical activity can produce the same effect.

—— Strenuous activity burns 300 to 800 calories per hour: running, swimming, skiing and heavy physical labour.
—— Vigorous activity burns 200 to 300 calories per hour: golfing, cycling, riding, dancing and heavy housework.
—— Moderate activity burns 100 to 200 calories per hour: gardening, walking, and ordinary housework.

Physical exercise is also known to relieve boredom, a prime antecedent for eating, and a competing response to eating.

Researchers at New Mexico State University have found

that a weight-control programme that emphasizes both changes in eating habits and exercise is more successful than a programme that focuses on eating habits alone.

As with intake of calories, it is wise to plan your weekly exercise schedule.

Step 2: Gaining Access to the Unconscious

Use the procedures taught in Chapter 3 to put yourself into a hypnotic state.

Step 3: Self-suggestion (Positive Thinking) and Success Visualization

Have a clear mental image in your mind, of yourself standing on the scale and the scale registering the weight you wish to be. See yourself looking the way you would like to look with the weight off those parts of the body you want the weight to be off. Then, silently but believingly, give yourself the following suggestions:

> *This is the way I would look, when I have attained this weight. I will be able to maintain it, I will find myself eating just enough to maintain my weight at the weight I would like to be. Until I do attain this weight I will find I have less and less desire to eat between meals. Also, I will find I will be content with smaller meals. Day by day, I will desire low-calorie, healthy foods, and this will replace the high calorie foods, the rich foods, I have eaten in the past. As I lose weight and approach closer and closer to the weight I wish to be, I will find myself growing stronger and fitter, healthier and healthier.*

Repeat two or three times per day.

Step 4: Real Life Activity

Parts of this step are already given in Step 1 above, as the flow appears to be there. Additionally, the two 'real life' activities given in Chapter 3 (How to Keep Your Spirits High and Controlling Your Environment) are very appropriate here. For now, I wish to describe several variations of the two 'real life' activities as they are specifically relevant to the problem in hand.

Motivation to Weight Loss

Firstly, as Dr Mary Harris of Stanford University suggests,

look at an unattractive picture of your 'fat' self in a bathing suit, the you you hate people to see, whenever you are tempted by inappropriate food. Ask yourself, 'Does this have to be me?'

And secondly, list on a piece of paper all the reasons why you want to lose weight (e.g. in order to look attractive, for health purposes, because overweight is socially unacceptable, etc) and carry it always with you. Each time you are not in the right mood, reflect on what you have written there.

Controlling Your Environment

When an obese person goes shopping, she tends to buy too many high-calorie items. To counteract this, it is wise to prepare a list beforehand, take only enough money to purchase the items you have on your list, and shop when you really do not have time to shop. If possible, do not take your children with you. Children tend to nag for sweets.

Whenever possible, avoid places where a lot of high-calorie foods are readily available (e.g., parties, sporting events, etc). But, if that is not possible, try imagining as vividly as possible a situation in which someone is likely to offer you a fattening food. Then, practise assertive statements, e.g., 'No thank you. I am on a diet.' Repeat this several times until you are able to say it naturally and comfortably. *If you wish, you can also carry out this exercise after hypnotic state has been accomplished.*

Many obese people have an uncontrollable urge to eat, eat and eat. What typically happens is that it is the snack they sneak in between meals that derails their efforts to lose weight. If this happens, try this:

Write down the names of foods which produce this kind of effect upon you. Pick up one and put it in front of you. Gaze at it steadily for one minute and say something like 'I am not going to be controlled by such a nothing like you' several times. Afterward, throw the food into the rubbish bin. Now, imagine yourself filled with pride, beaming at your accomplishment at resisting temptation. You are feeling wonderful inside. Imagine friends and family around you patting you on the back. That special someone says, 'I knew you could do it.' Repeat the exercise with other kinds of food.

In a novel experiment, Pennsylvania State University

researchers investigated the eating behaviour of obese and non-obese people in a fast-food restaurant. Results showed that obese people took more bites but chewed their food less thoroughly and more quickly than non-obese eaters. Since quick eating appears to have the effect of inducing a person to eat more than she should, it is wise to take smaller bites and chew more thoroughly and slowly.

7.

Banish That Smoking Habit

Basically, there are two ways that you can banish your smoking habit: all at once (sometimes called 'going cold turkey') and gradually.

Cold Turkey
The 'cold turkey' method is especially indicated for those who have a strong competitive spirit, believe that they can do it and are not deluded about the dangers of smoking.

In my opinion, this method should always be tried out first; and if it does not work, one can always turn to the other method. You have nothing to gain but your health.

Consider the Following
1. Get rid of all your cigarettes, together with ashtrays, cigarette packs, matches, lighter and if possible, other things which remind you of your old smoking habit. If there are things which you associate with smoking, but do not want to get rid of (e.g. furniture), rearrange them so that they become less familiar.
2. Tell everyone who is likely to comment on your effort (e.g. your smoking spouse, friends, the tobacconist's where you previously purchased cigarettes, etc.) that you have made up your mind to quit smoking. The anticipated loss of face if you return to your smoking habit may act as a deterrent not to smoke.
3. Do not fall into the trap of wanting to test your will power. Do not buy cigarettes and, as much as possible, avoid people who smoke. Structure your time to engage in non-smoking activities e.g. concerts, evening courses, etc.
4. Put a 'No Smoking' sign in the living room and learn to use assertive statements to ask guests to refrain from smoking.

In other places, learn to refuse offers of cigarettes graciously.
5. When you feel the urge to smoke, carry out the 'Thought Stopping and Thought Switching' strategy. It consists of three steps.

Step A
Mentally get hold of the urge by fully experiencing it.

Step B
Suddenly – shout mentally '*stop*'; imagine a red traffic light flashing very very vividly in your mind's eye; and tense some parts of your body slightly.

Step C
Make an effort of the will to switch your attention either to a pleasant thought or image or activity. For example:

—— The thought of winning a £100,000 lottery.
—— The image of a sexy girl (or a muscular man).
—— A pleasant activity which is incompatible with smoking such as taking some fresh air, eating, physical exercise.

The last activity (exercise) is particularly recommended by The American Cancer Society, which asserts that it is very helpful in relieving the immediate feeling of irritation many smokers feel when they miss a cigarette.

Read the rest of this chapter. You may find additional strategies that may apply to your situation.

Gradual Withdrawal Method
Step 1: Making Concrete Formulation of Goal
Apply the tips given in Chapter 2 with special reference to smoking rate. More specifically, each time you smoke, make note of it. Pay special attention to the various situations under which it occurs and its consequences. At night, before going to bed, sum them up. Carry this out for one week before attempting to change your smoking habit and chart the results.

Gradually reduce the cigarette intake (for example, Week 1 goal–25 cigarettes smoked; Week 2 Goal–20 cigarettes smoked; Week 3 Goal–15 cigarettes smoked; etc.).

Step 2: Gaining Access to the Unconscious

Use the procedures given in Chapter 3 to put yourself into hypnotic state.

Step 3: Self-suggestion (Positive Thinking)

Once or twice per day suggest the following statements sincerely and emphatically.

1. I am that much closer to lung cancer.
2. It has been estimated that 200,000 to 300,000 deaths per year occur prematurely because of cigarette smoking.
3. According to Dr Weeks from University of Edinburgh, there is evidence that cigarette smoking encourages the formation of generalized atherosclerosis (hardening and thickening of the blood vessel walls).
4. There is no such thing as a 'safe level' of smoking.
5. I feel terrible that the kids might pick up my habit.

If you wish, you can also construct other suggestions you find appropriate. Do not hesitate. Go ahead and experiment. Your life is in your hands.

The above-mentioned suggestions can also be used as a part of Step 4 in the following way. Write down statements 1-5 on small index cards and post them on the places where you usually smoke (e.g. TV room, work place, etc). Make them as conspicuous as possible.

Step 4: Real Life Activity

Much of what has been said in Chapters 3 and 5 are directly relevant here. (Of course, some of the tips may require a slight modification.) For now, I wish to suggest some variations which are especially applicable to the problem at hand.

To increase your desire to stop smoking, you may make a formal contract with yourself to the effect that if you exceed your maximum daily intake by a certain number of cigarettes, a penalty is to follow, and ask a trusted person (e.g. your neighbour) to witness it. It may also be useful to allow a loved one to assess you each time he or she witnesses your lighting up. The contract may take the form of that given below.

A Contingency Contract for Stopping Smoking

I, Mr [name] from [address] hereby agree to abide by the following conditions:

During the period of A to B, my highest daily rate would be 20 cigarettes.

During the period of B to C, my highest daily rate would be 15 cigarettes.

During the period of C to D, my highest daily rate would be 10 cigarettes.

During the period of D to E, my highest daily rate would be 5 cigarettes.

During the period of E to ..., my highest daily rate would be 0 cigarettes.

Each time I exceed my daily rate by one cigarette, I shall send a £5.00 note to my mother-in-law.

E.g. If during the period of A to B I smoke 25 cigarettes per day, I will have to send £25.00 to my mother-in-law.

Signed: ....
.... (Witness)
Date: ....

Secondly, try to find some people after whom you would like to model yourself and who are either non-smokers or ex-smokers. Each time you feel tempted by a cigarette advertisement or other similar event, say the following silently and sincerely to yourself, 'These people have exceptional qualities and have made remarkable achievements. To hell with the erroneous belief that smoking is a prerequisite to maturity, popularity and success.'

Lastly, each time you find yourself reaching for a cigarette, break it into two and wait for ten seconds before putting it into your mouth. This strategy is ideal for the type of smoker who does not even realize the cigarette is in his mouth. In this way, his smoking is no longer an automatic subconscious activity; it has become a consciously deliberated act, which is easier to control. Also, since smoking will become more of an effort, it will lose some of its attractive value.

8.

Smash the Sleep Barrier

There are four common barriers to sleep, and by smashing them you can expect to have a restful sleep. A variation of Step 2-4 is appropriate for smashing Sleep Barrier 1. A variation of Step 2 alone will do for smashing Sleep Barrier 2. And a variation of Step 4 is suitable for smashing Sleep Barrier 3 and 4.

Sleep Barrier 1
The fear of losing conscious control, of surrendering oneself to the inner darkness are common among people for whom getting to sleep is a nightly and often losing battle.

To smash this barrier, select either one of the following three strategies.

Strategy 1: Paradoxical Intention
This strategy will be described fully under 'sleep barrier 4'.

Strategy 2: Rational Emotive Therapy
Find out several basic reasons why Sleep Barrier 1 is irrational (e.g. during sleep, my unconscious mind will take care of me; no healthy person has ever died of sleeping). Prior to sleep at night, relax your body and calm your mind through the hypnotic relaxation exercise to be described under Sleep Barrier 2' Next, read these reasons emphatically to yourself three times. As the days go, more relevant ideas may pop to your mind and consequently you may delete some of the statements you originally constructed and add new ones (e.g. a good night's sleep will recharge my battery, increase my vitality and improve my performance in every way). After several days, the ideas usually start to sink in.

Strategy 3: Praying
This strategy is usually useful for those who have religious

faith. However, even those who do not have any religious faith frequently find it useful to read slowly some passages from the Bible prior to sleep (which is a form of prayer). One of the most useful biblical passages is Psalms 18:22.

> The Lord is my fort where I can enter and be safe; no one can follow me in and slay me. He is a rugged mountain where I hide; he is my saviour, a rock where none can reach me, and a tower of safety. He is my shield. He is like the strong horn of a mighty fighting bull.

Again, after several days the ideas usually start to sink in.

Sleep Barrier 2

Anxiety and tension are among the most significant characteristics of poor sleepers.

To smash this barrier, carry out the following hypnotic relaxation exercise (or any other which you find useful) for about ten minutes immediately prior to sleep.

> *Imagine a beautiful lake. Allow the image to develop and take its form. There is a full moon. You can see the light of the moon reflected in the water of the lake. The waves are moving slowly and unobtrusively. So quiet, peaceful and calm. As you experience this feeling, let every part of your body relax, one at a time. Accentuate the environment with all your senses. Smell the flowers and listen to the sound of the forest. You are actually there.*

The logic of this exercise has been described by Dr Bootzin from North-western University as follows.

> Muscle relaxation is associated with the onset of sleep and some researchers have held that muscle relaxation induces sleep. One form of evidence for this conclusion is that people deprived of sleep for more than twenty-four hours are unable to stay awake while completely relaxed. Since one might consider insomniacs, in some sense deprived of sleep, then it follows that if they can be taught to completely relax while in bed, sleep should come naturally.

Sleep Barrier 3

The ruminating thoughts you have while tossing and turning (especially if they are about your problems) may actually keep you from sleeping.

To smash this barrier, try 'Thought Stopping and Thought Switching'. It consists of three steps.

Step A
Mentally get hold of the thoughts by fully experiencing them.

Step B
Suddenly, shout mentally '*stop*', imagine a red traffic light flashing very very vividly in your mind's eye and tense some parts of your body slightly.

Step C
Make an effort of the will to switch your attention either to a pleasant thought (e.g. the thought of winning £100,000 in a lottery) or a pleasant image (e.g. the image of a lake in Sleep Barrier 2 section).

One or two applications of this technique is usually sufficient to get rid of the undesirable thoughts. If they return, repeat the procedure.

Sleep Barrier 4
This sleep barrier is rightly called 'performance anxiety'. That is to say, the person in question is unable to sleep because, in a nut shell, he forces (wills) himself to sleep.

To my knowledge, the best strategy for overcoming performance anxiety is a technique developed by Dr Frankl from Vienna. It is known as 'Paradoxical Intention'.

Essentially, the person in question is instructed to make fun of his sleeping problem and do exactly the opposite, namely, to force himself not to sleep.

A lucid illustration of this technique has been reported by Professor Gambrill from University of California.

Mr M, a 43-year-old male, complained of severe sleep disturbance of ten years' duration and had made a superficial suicide attempt occasioned by financial difficulties. He was referred by his psychiatrist, who felt that continued use of sleeping medication was neither effective nor advisable. Mr M. was obsessed with the idea that he to have some sleep. He was informed that the reason he could not sleep was that he was trying too hard. As expected, he countered this by pointing out that it was reasonable that he should be concerned, since his lack of sleep interfered with his life. The counsellor suggested that he might overcome his concern by doing just the opposite of what he wanted, that is, to try and stay awake all night. The next morning the client informed the counsellor that he had tried this and, in an 'I told you so' attitude, informed the counsellor that he had not slept all night. He was congratulated for following instructions and was asked to do the same the following night. The next morning the client informed the counsellor that he had again tried to stay awake but had fallen asleep for a couple of hours. According to the hospital records he had slept for seven hours. He continued the procedure and reported six and a half to seven hours of sleep per night.

So that often elusive commodity, sound, restful sleep, can sometimes be captured by devious means, and sometimes by the simple application of sound, common sense principles. I wish you success in breaking down the barriers.

9.

Tips from a Former Stutterer

I used to stutter very badly. At its acute stage, not only did I not talk properly, but I was not able to utter the intended word at all. I can still remember very vividly an incident, during my teens, when I could not answer at all, on hearing my name called from a register at school. My stuttering years are indeed the most traumatic, embarrassing and humiliating experience of my life. After a long and arduous struggle, I am now capable of speaking as well as anyone else, and even running highly successful public speaking classes.

In retrospect, what I have done to help myself involves a combination of Step 3 and Step 4 in the model for the effective use of self-hypnosis. I would like to describe them briefly for your benefit. I hope you will find them useful.

One of the basic reasons why I stuttered is because I hated myself and had the uncanny habit of constant self-criticism, especially of the way I spoke. I was afraid my utterance would be a nuisance to others. (Interestingly enough, I did not stutter when I was not conscious of my speaking e.g., when I was speaking alone or talking to my dog.)

Slowly and painfully, I learned to *be fair to myself*. I started to accept the fact that I am unique, and that what I do is as worthwhile as what anyone else does. I learned, when I spoke, to concentrate exclusively on the ideas and the listener and *lost myself in them*. I understood what the famous psychiatrist, Dr V.E. Frankl has called 'Self Transcendence'.

Learning to be Assertive

It needs to be emphasized that I did not try to be aggressive, if by aggression we mean 'lacking respect for our neighbour's feeling and value'. I was merely trying to *be assertive*. More specifically, I was demanding, or better still, claiming my basic rights: the right to enjoy popularity and respect, the right to make mistakes and improve myself, the right to value myself aright, and above all, the right to speak in any pleasant manner I choose. I realized that no one has the right to make me feel small and insecure, not. even my parents and employers.

Assertiveness is indispensable for a stutterer, because, as a stutterer talks in the defensive, he will find it more and more difficult to breathe, until, in the end, he is completely trapped in the vicious circle. It is therefore crucial that a stutterer *must never talk in the defensive*. He should learn to pause and think what he is going to say, and when he is convinced that the truth is on his side, he should speak freely, without any inhibitions.

Demosthenes knew this point well. He had launched a frontal attack on his stuttering by practising speaking with pebbles in his mouth. At the end, he became the greatest orator the Greek nation ever produced.

The only way a stutterer can speak assertively is by doing it *slowly and with great mental effort*. Speak as if the listener has come to borrow money from you. Have no fear that this will offend him. The only time he will feel offended is when you lose your decisiveness.

Improving Your Self Image

I have mentioned that one of the basic reasons I stuttered is due to my dislike of myself. This, and other erroneous thinking are the crux of the problem. For my part, they have to do with my implicit (unconscious) belief at that time that 'if I speak fluently as anyone else, the listener will be hurt'. This realization did not come spontaneously. It came only after a long period of reflection. I used to spend 10-15 minutes every day for self-examination (to correct wrong thinking and discover my true personality). Now that I have overcome my problem, I can affirm, from personal experience, the truth of Dr Ladell's remark that 'Hidden behind the tongue-tied contortions of the stammerer there almost always is a worthwhile and efficient personality.'

Many books contain strategies for creating a better self-image, etc, but, unfortunately, most of them are laborious and impracticable. A method which I find useful is the Mirror

Exercise (see Chapter 13). Here, a slight modification will be in order. After you have intimately been in touch with your image in the mirror, say,

> *I am a normal person. Each day, as I stand up here, I'll have a healthier and healthier view of myself. I know that I deserve it. I know that I have the right to speak as well as everybody else. As my thinking gets more and more logical, naturally my speaking style will improve. This is because my way of speaking is a reflection of my own attitudes and beliefs, which are of my own making.*

Persistence

It took me several months to achieve a substantial gain and several years to overcome it completely. If you are a heavy stutterer, the same may apply to you. To increase my *persistence*, I used to post the following poem (by Calvin Coolidge) on the wall of my study room.

> Nothing in the world
> can take the place of persistence,
> Talent will not;
> nothing is more common than
> unsuccessful men with talent.
> Genius will not;
> unrewarded genius is almost a proverb.
> Education will not;
> the world is full of educated derelicts.
> Persistence and determination
> alone are omnipotent.
> The slogan 'Press On' has solved
> and always will solve
> the problems of the human race.

Stuttering has been the most difficult and painful battle of my life. But, I have gained victory over it. If you are willing to put in the same effort, I have not the slightest doubt that you will do too.

10.

Marriage: a Four Week Programme to Improve Your Relationship

According to a recent report, there has been a continual upward trend in the rate of divorce in the United States with an increase of 80 per cent in the past ten years alone.

Factors related to the increase in divorce probably include the increasing acceptance of divorce as normal, the increase in alternatives available to women and the rising standard of expectation for happiness in marriage.

It is clear that after a couple marries, a variety of types of interactions and potential pleasures and annoyances from these interactions are likely to occur.

As time goes by, and as events change, these sources will also change, requiring a continual rematching between interest in certain pleasures and the degree to which they are offered. Many couples cannot manage this matching process.

Professor Gambrill from the University of California has defined a good marriage 'as one in which satisfaction is expressed by both participants, in which each person mediates important positive events for the other, and in which pleasant events exchanged clearly outweigh the unpleasant.'

In what follows, you will find a four-week programme to achieve this goal. It requires the co-operation of both spouses and consists of four procedures.

Satisfaction Procedure
Before proceeding with any programme whatsoever, jot down as specifically (concretely) as possible ten 'satisfactions' currently received from and ten 'satisfactions' currently given to your spouse. Thus, for example:

—— *Instead of saying:*
'My wife is quite sexy these days'
Say:
'Twice per week, she sleeps without her clothes on.'
—— *Instead of saying:*
'Sometimes, my husband is quite good.'
Say:
'He brings flowers home every week.'
—— *Instead of saying:*
'I occasionally do my husband a favour.'
Say:
'I give him a good night kiss three times per week.'

The major objective of this procedure is to increase awareness of satisfactions already exchanged. This usually has the effect of enabling the participants to see things in their true perspective, without magnifying their difficulties, without allowing them to get out of proportion. A typical comment would be, 'My husband is not too bad after all. He sometimes does show me his love'; or, 'I am not too good either. What have I done to please her?' This procedure will also discourage the assumption that each already knows what the other thinks, and encourage reticent partners to share what they think. It is therefore an essential starting point for change.

Perfect Marriage Procedure
Jot down 'interactions' that would represent your idea of an ideal marriage for each of the nine 'problem areas' below as 'honestly' as possible.

1. Household responsibilities
2. Rearing of children (if any)
3. Social activities
4. Money
5. Communication
6. Sex
7. Academic or occupational progress
8. Personal independence
9. Spouse independence

Examples
   4. Money:

- I will be glad if my wife does not spend more than £30 per week for clothes.
5. Communication:
  - I will be delighted if my husband spends at least half-an-hour per day conversing with me after work instead of watching TV.
  - I will be happy if my wife listens to me when I speak.
6. Sex:
  - I will be pleased if we can make love three times per week.

A rule that needs to be followed here is that of 'reasonableness' or 'attainability'. This is due to the fact that by its very nature, marriage gives rise to both blessings and restrictions, and that it is necessary to accept this fact if one wants to enhance marital interaction. Thus, for example, to expect your spouse to continually please you without any effort on your part to reciprocate, will clearly lead to problems.

In the first week, each must try to satisfy the other's desires in relation to problem areas 1-3. In the second and third weeks, work with problem areas 4-6, and then with problem areas 7-9, and in the last week, as the responses start to habituate, it should not be too difficult to work with all problem areas. Occasionally, if it is difficult to satisfy a desire totally (e.g. 'I want my husband to relax during sex'), it would be acceptable to satisfy it *partially*.

Spend at least half-an-hour each evening filling in the 'Marital Happiness Scale' (shown on page 68) and discussing what you are doing. When you do this, take care not to resurrect 'past conflicts'. For example, a statement such as, 'You left dirty dishes in the sink two days ago because this is just what your mother did' must never be uttered, since it tends to generate harmful arguments. Instead, each partner must be prepared to forgive, be open-minded and discuss things calmly and rationally. The discussion has to be conducted with the sole aim of finding out how each partner can satisfy the other to a fuller extent. Negatives that bother a spouse can be addressed within this emphasis, by simply learning to identify behaviours to be encouraged.

Appreciation Procedure

Always carry a small piece of paper with you and jot down the novel, unusual, unscheduled satisfaction(s) your partner gives you (e.g. the unscheduled cleaning of the house). During the 'discussion time' in the evening, let him/her know how much you appreciate what he/she has done.

Positive Outlook

Each time you make a 'negative' statement, add a positive one. Or, better still, learn to criticize in a constructive fashion. For example:

> *Instead of saying:*
> 'That was a dumb thing to say.'
> *Say:*
> 'That may be true, but did you ever view it from this perspective?'

Each time your spouse violates this rule, gently remind him/her that you will not respond unless he/she has added a positive statement or reformulated the statement.

Measure Your Improvement

After four weeks, the clients typically report a substantial amount of improvement in their marital happiness as shown by the Marital Happiness Scale scores. Also, the effort is experienced as more and more natural, effortless, habitual and enjoyable.

As with any other endeavour, some initial difficulty is likely to be encountered. This, however, is not a sign to give up. Rather, it is a sign to press on and continue the good effort. Remember the poem given at the end of Chapter 8.

	totally unhappy					so so				totally happy
	▼					▼				▼
Household responsibilities	1	2	3	4	5	5.5	6	7	8	9	10
Rearing of children	1	2	3	4	5	5.5	6	7	8	9	10
Social activities	1	2	3	4	5	5.5	6	7	8	9	10
Money	1	2	3	4	5	5.5	6	7	8	9	10
Communication	1	2	3	4	5	5.5	6	7	8	9	10
Sex	1	2	3	4	5	5.5	6	7	8	9	10
Occupational or academic progress	1	2	3	4	5	5.5	6	7	8	9	10
Personal independence	1	2	3	4	5	5.5	6	7	8	9	10
Spouse independence	1	2	3	4	5	5.5	6	7	8	9	10

Instructions

Put a circle around the number which best depicts your marital state for each of the nine areas listed above. Thus, for example, if your spouse demands an absolutely unreasonable form of independence (e.g. the right to have an affair), you may circle 1 on the last item. Later, as he/she starts to assume marital responsibility in this matter, you may circle 2, 3, 4 or 5, depending on the degree. And still later, when you start to feel happy about his/her behaviour, you may decide to circle 6, 7, 8, etc.

The Marital Happiness Scale is the measure of your progress during the 4 week period.

By filling it in carefully and using it as a focal point for discussion, you will be able to see how your relationship goes. Furthermore, every experienced clinician recognizes that it is not uncommon (in marital conflict) to find one or both parties behave childishly. The M.H.S. can here serve as a brake, to remind them that they need to handle the problem rationally and with a clear mind. E. Berne, the author of *Games People Play* (Penguin, 1970) will, I think, interpret this as a transition from child ego state to adult ego state.

The following exercise may be useful. Once or twice per day, relax your mind and body through the hypnotic relaxation procedures described in Chapter 3. Then give yourself the following suggestion with great faith and conviction.

I totally forgive anyone who needs my forgiveness, both now and in the past; I fully and completely forgive. I am totally forgiven by anyone who needs to forgive me, both now and in the past; I am totally and fully forgiven. Anger serves no purpose. It has nothing to do with being a happy, fulfilled person. The world and the people in it do not have to succumb to my wish. Others have the right to be different from what I would prefer.

11.

Overcoming Sexual Inadequacy

Most forms of sexual inadequacy are psychologically caused. For example, the man who enters sex with the thought, 'Wouldn't it be awful if I became so tense or anxious during sex that I lost my erection' may thereby engender sufficient anxiety to suppress all sexual feeling. This is called *performance anxiety*. The sexual anorexia of many a frigid female may be traced to formative encounters with insensitive men who provided crudeness and vulgarity in place of tenderness and consideration. Many premature ejaculators have a history of intercourse in situations in which they have had to be concerned about 'discovery'. 'Indeed', says Dr A. Runciman from San Fernando Valley State University, 'the vast majority of sexual dysfunctions in both sexes result from psychological rather than organic factors'.

The importance of psychological factors, however, does not imply that physical factors cannot have a profound effect on the sexual performance. For example, diabetes mellitus may decrease potency in males. Ingestion of oestrogen in males for treatment of carcinoma of the prostate can markedly decrease sexual interest. Certain types of oral contraceptives may decrease sexual interest in women. Therefore, before trying out the tips given in this article, it is wise to rule out the possible influence of a variety of physical factors through a complete medical check up and a medical history, including diet and a description of any medication currently taken.

In what follows, the management of three major forms of sexual inadequacy i.e. impotence (men's failure to attain or maintain an erection long enough for full coitus); frigidity (women's failure to attain orgasm) and premature ejaculation will be discussed.

Common Myths Corrected

As you think, so shall you feel (and what we feel, influences the way we behave). This wisdom has been expressed by various thinkers as follows.

—— Ralph Waldo Emerson:
'A man is what he thinks about all day long.'
—— Marcus Aurelius:
'A man's life is what his thoughts make it.'
—— Norman Vincent Peale:
'Change your thoughts and you change your worlds.'
—— The Bible:
'For as he thinketh in his heart, so is he.' (Proverbs 23:7)
—— Benjamin Whichcote:
'None can do a man so much harm as he doeth himself.'

Applying this hint specifically to the problems of sexual inadequacy, an irresistable conclusion follows. There is good reason to believe that sexual misconceptions underlie most forms of impotence, frigidity and premature ejaculation, and that by correcting these misconceptions, an improvement can be expected to occur.

In what follows, the most common misconceptions about sexual acts and desires will be stated; each of them is to be followed by a description of the corresponding truth.

—— *Myth 1*
I am a real man only when I am sexually responsive to all women and capable of immediate sexual arousal.
The truth
Various sensitizing factors such as poor diet, fatigue from overwork, selection of distracting environments for attempted sexual interactions, poor health and alcohol problems can all decrease sexual response and interest.
—— *Myth 2*
My penis is small. Thus, I am not going to be able to satisfy my partner. (Or, my husband's penis is small. Thus, he is not going to be able to satisfy me.)

The truth

There is no correlation whatsoever between genital size and the pleasure your partner experiences.

—— *Myth 3*

Sex is a kind of dirty word.

The truth

Sex and sexual activities are natural, essential and a wonderful part of living.

—— *Myth 4*

Normal sexual intercourse is a manifestation of a male physically dominating a female, solely for the male's satisfaction.

The truth

A woman intensely wants and needs penetration to feel fulfilled.

—— *Myth 5*

A good woman does not want sexual intercourse, or only wants it for procreation purposes.

The truth

A healthy woman has just as strong a need and drive for intercourse as a healthy man.

—— *Myth 6*

Taking visual delight in the nude figure of my wife is sinful.

The truth

A wife wishes her husband to enjoy the sight of her body.

—— *Myth 7*

An erection should occur automatically. It can be willed.

The truth

For people in their forties and more, some type of overt stimulation is needed to produce an erection. To will an erection is impossible.

—— *Myth 8*

Personal gratification in and from intercourse is selfishly wrong.

The truth

The only way for my wife (husband) to be completely satisfied sexually is for me to concentrate on my selfish desire.

—— *Myth 9*
I am frigid because I am capable of achieving only manually induced clitorial orgasms.
The truth
'Penile-vaginal intercourse may abet orgasm through providing indirect stimulation for the clitoral-situated genital corpuscles; or in some copulative positions, it may result in direct stimulation for the clitoris itself. No matter: the female orgasm is still mainly clitoral and not vaginal. So-called vaginal orgasm, therefore, is a myth.'
(A. Ellis, the author of *The American Sexual Tragedy*.)
—— *Myth 10*
Once I get married, everything will work itself out.
The truth
As in any other endeavour, there is no gain without work. If you wish to have a fulfilling relationship with your spouse, you have to work for it.

In many cases, the correction of misconceptions is sufficient for effecting lasting change. Occasionally, however, a stronger action is needed. It is not enough to understand the correct information intellectually. Rather, you need to spend 5-10 minutes per day to reflect on the correct information until you also emotionally accept it. An example of this approach has been reported by Drs Rathus and Nevid as follows.

One twenty-two-year old graduate student in psychology wrote several such statements down on small index cards and placed them by her tooth brush in her bathroom. Each time she went to brush her teeth she read the cards to herself in random order. She was instructed to be certain that she read them emphatically to herself. Several times she dropped a statement or two and added others as new, relevant ideas occurred to her. She reported that they began to 'sink in' after a week had passed.

The statements can also be treated as *self-suggestion*, in which case it is a good idea to put yourself first into the hypnotic state (see Chapter 3) before suggesting them to yourself.

Graded Sexual Assignments
When the impotence and frigidity are serious, the procedure described in the last section needs to be combined with a

'graded sexual assignment' procedure. It proceeds as follows.

At the beginning, it may be helpful to take a bath together and to give each other a complete body massage while nude; but not to touch the breasts or genitals (or attempt intercourse). That is to say, refrain from all activity which tends to produce tension and anxiety.

This procedure serves to eliminate the embarrassment the partners may feel about each other. Also, it will enable them to find out each other's erotic parts other than the breasts and the genitals. Do not be ashamed to ask your partner what he/she likes. The person who is doing the touching receives instructions from his/her partner such as up, down, left, higher, faster, stronger, etc. At all times each partner must let his/her body feel the pleasure of being caressed.

Since penetration is not to be attempted, many men who suffer from performance anxiety (the fear that he will not be able to satisfy the partner sexually) are able to relax, enjoy and achieve erection at this point.

Occasionally, it is useful to add the use of assertive statements at this point, since assertive statements tend to decrease anxiety. This is particularly necessary when the male partner has an unnecessarily servile and deferential attitude towards his spouse (maybe, because of his formative training) and is therefore unable to make sexual advances. In such a case, it is wise to jot down the speech beforehand and rehearse it in imagination during hypnotic state until it is experienced as natural and real. An example of such a speech has been reported by Dr Lazarus from The State University.

> I was raised by my mother to bottle up my feelings, especially in relation to women. In thinking this attitude over, I now realize that this is crazy and even dishonest. I feel, for instance, that if I resent the fact that you turn to your father for advice in matters about which I have more knowledge than he, I ought to express my resentment instead of hiding it from you. I feel that when you order me about and treat me like a child, I ought to tell you how I really feel about it instead of acting like an obedient puppy dog. And most important of all, when you go ahead and make plans for me without consulting me, and especially when you yell at me in front of your parents, maybe I should quit acting as if I didn't mind and let you know how strongly I really react inside. What I am getting at is simply that in spite of my love and affection for you, I would really rather be unmarried than be a henpecked husband like my father.

Once the couple is able to carry out the first step without any anxiety, some hugging and kissing can be added.

Once this step, too, is mastered, genital caressing can be added. At this point, most men and women feel aroused. If not, persist until it happens.

The fourth step is sometimes called the 'teasing' technique. Each partner tries to arouse the other through genital caressing and once this is achieved, he/she stops. Then, he/she starts again. This procedure serves to teach the partners that erection and excitement, once they are lost, can be gained again.

In the fifth step, the wife is to assume the 'female superior sitting position' (i.e. the male lies on his back and the female sits over him) and places the penis at the entrance of the vagina. This position is particularly useful for females who are fearful of male dominance. It helps her to feel more in command and gives her permission to express her sexual strivings. Also, it is less likely than other postures to stimulate the prematurely ejaculating male to orgasm. It is therefore a good position from which to learn to control one's ejaculatory behaviour.

And finally, slow pelvic thrusting can be attempted.

The steps mentioned above are not to be regarded as a strait jacket. Any sequence can be tried out as long as it leads to enjoyable, full intercourse.

With a slight modification, these steps are also useful for the management of premature ejaculation. In this endeavour, each step can be performed, but only when ejaculation does not occur. Slowly, as the male partner gains more and more control over his ejaculatory behaviour, the couple can proceed toward the sixth step (i.e. towards a more exciting step). If in the process, however, the male partner feels that he cannot hold it any longer, the squeeze method can be carried out. In this method, the female places her thumb on the frenulum and her first and second fingers on the dorsal surface of the penis and applies pressure by squeezing the thumb and the first two fingers together for about three to four seconds. With sufficient pressure, the male will lose the urge to ejaculate and lose part of his erection.

Concluding Remarks

As in any other learning endeavour, the progress may not always be smooth. There will be ups and downs. This, however, is not a sign at all to get discouraged. Continue the effort day by day, week by week, until you achieve your goal. A case reported by Dr Lazarus in his famous book *Behaviour Therapy and Beyond* (McGraw, 1971) is probably worthwhile quoting at length.

> You will recall that both Julie and I were sceptical of the sexual program you advised. All the same, we went through the paces. I think I went slower than anybody. In the first few times we just sort of cuddled in the living room. In less than five minutes I became tense so we quit. A few nights after that we were, as the teenagers would put it, 'making out', and I had my hand inside Julie's bra. I didn't feel tense but neither was I aroused. I don't remember exactly how soon afterwards – about a week I'd guess – we'd go through the motions of intercourse with our clothes on in the living room and I'd become semierect. It got to the point where we would masturbate each other in the living room to climax, but in the bedroom nothing would happen. I am sure this was because the bedroom reminded me of all my past failures. In fact, I think it had something to do with beds. It had gotten to the point where I could perform just fine on the living room rug, when Julie surprised me by buying one of those sofa-bed arrangements. At first I was impotent until we moved back onto the floor. In fact, one night we were in bed and kind of stroking each other; as usual nothing happened, so I suggested that we move onto the rug. There I was fine and we had intercourse. We used to kid each other about this floor angle, but it sort of bothered me. We overcame this problem in two ways. First, we would stimulate each other in bed, knowing full well that if nothing happened we could always move onto the floor. This was most reassuring. Secondly, we would make love in bed in the early morning when I tended to have an erection anyway.

12.

Social Skill Training

Essentially, social skill training is indicated for those who feel a need to enhance their self worth and ability to better survive in a socialized society. Upon analysis, these people tend to fall into two categories: the aggressive and the submissive. (In my experience, the latter are more likely to come to a Social Skill Training Group than the former.)

The aggressive person puts down, hurts or humiliates people. Goals are achieved at the expense of causing bad feelings in others. The aggressive person is avoided by other people.

The submissive person, on the other hand, allows others to choose for him. He does not achieve what he really wants. His reactions indicate that he is in the wrong and that the other person is right. The submissive person avoids other people.

By contrast, the socially skilled person is able to defend his rights and the rights of others. He behaves and speaks in a way which makes others take his ideas into account. Yet, he cares about other people's feelings and knows how to express himself in as positive way as possible.

Cultural Reasons for Aggressiveness and Submissiveness

Aggressiveness and submissiveness can easily be caused by the uncritical acceptance of irrational beliefs or myths. Some of these myths are quite pervasive in Western culture and are worth while stating here.

1. *The Myth of 'Modesty'*
   This says, in effect, that one should not acknowledge compliments from others.
2. *The 'Crystal Ball' Myth*
   This says, in effect, that others should know what it is you would like.
3. *The Myth of the 'Nice Person'*

This says, in effect, that one has to please everyone in any circumstances. It is better simply to let things go and not say anything. No matter what happens, one should never criticize others or complain.

4. *The Myth of 'Perfectionism'*
This say, in effect, that to be turned down is awful. One has to perform perfectly in any circumstances (i.e. 'I must never make mistakes').

5. *The Myth of 'Masculinity'*
This says, in effect, that it is unmanly to express compliments and emotions. To do so is childish. If a man is going to make it, he has got to be tough.

This is how you can put the newly acquired knowledge into practice. Write the statements which contradict the above-mentioned myths (e.g. To err is only human. I have the right to have a good life. The true gentleman is able to express his real feelings, etc.) on small index cards and place them by your toothbrush in your bathroom. Each time you go to brush your teeth, read the cards emphatically to yourself in random order. As new, relevant ideas occur to you, drop a statement or two and add others (e.g. add, To be able to graciously acknowledge admirable qualities in oneself is a virtue. There are only a few telepathists around these days, etc.). Usually, after a week has passed, these statements begin to sink in.

You can also put yourself into the hypnotic state (see chapter 2) and suggest these statements to yourself when you are there.

Rehearsal Desensitization
The basic technique used in social skill training is 'rehearsal desensitization'. It consists of four steps.

First Step
Construct a hierarchy of social interactions in terms of the degree of anxiety or anger that situations induce. An example of such an hierarchy has been reported by Dr Lazarus.

A twenty-four-item hierarchy was constructed along a continuum of progressively more assertive behaviour in the presence of one other person. The *lower* end of the hierarchy consisted of such items as: maintaining eye contact with herself in a mirror while speaking and maintaining eye contact with the therapist while silent. *Middle* hierarchy items were: complaining to a waiter about food, and asking a stranger on the street for directions. *High* hierarchy items involved: expressing and defending an opinion, discussing a controversial topic, and expressing, in a loud, clear voice, a novel idea regarding teaching methodology to a supervisor.

Second Step

Put yourself into hypnotic state (see Chapter 3) and then rehearse in your imagination the situations inducing a small degree of anger or anxiety. Persist until the experience is felt as real, natural and effortless. In this connection it is worthwhile noting that Dr Maltz, the author of the best seller *Psycho-cybernetics* (Wilshire Books, 1967) has mentioned that one of the most effective ways of changing a person's behaviour is to have him imagine himself the way he wants to be, rather than thinking of himself the way he actually is.

Third Step

Strengthen the effect of the second step by going out to the real world and acting as if you have become your ideal self. Use all your will to this end.

It should be clear by now that this is Step 4 in the model for the effective use of self-hypnosis (the 'As If' Principle). Please see Chapter 13 for details.

Fourth Step

After you have mastered the above situations, higher-level scenes can be gradually tried out as in the second and third steps.

In your endeavour, some initial resistance is likely to be encountered, especially from those who do not enjoy seeing you becoming a full and complete being. This is not, however, a sign to give up. Continue the good effort day by day, week by week, month by month until you become the kind of person you wish to be.

Remember what Lao Tze has said, 'Take one step at a time. The journey of 1000 miles begins with one step' and what Waldo Emerson wrote, 'Beware of what you want because you will get it.'

Useful Assertive Statements

An assertive response is stated in a *polite* but *firm* manner. The individual is neither overaggressive nor oversubmissive. Some examples of assertive statements will be given below, and when the situation demands, it may be useful to incorporate them into your 'rehearsal desensitization' procedure.

—— Listen, we have been waiting for a while. Why don't you move to the end of the queue.

—— I would prefer to sit over here. Could we?

—— Hello. Haven't I seen you somewhere before?

—— I know you are late for your appointment, but I do not have time now to drive you over.

—— What is immature about not wanting to lend you money? (in reply to; 'You are really being immature.')

—— None for me. I really like the way my clothes look now that I have lost weight. (in reply to, 'You know how delicious my cake is. Just a small piece couldn't hurt. Let me cut you one'.)

—— I can see how you might feel that way, but ... (state the reasons of your disagreement).

—— Wait a minute (when someone interrupts you).

—— I am sorry (when you are at fault).

—— Thank you (when someone offers you a compliment).

—— Jim, will you give me a lift to the office in the morning?

—— Sorry, but I would not like to make a donation this time.

When not to be Assertive

The skill acquired through rehearsal desensitization must not be misused. The principle of 'reasonableness' has to be adhered to at all times. The skill should be used only when the time is right.

A direct demand, for example, is not recommended in the situations which would entail very negative consequences, (e.g. when the possibility of being fired from your job is prominent).

Similarly, if the annoyance is a minor one (or, when the other side is already very upset), it may be best for all concerned to remain quiet or to select another time to express oneself.

In such cases, try to use *subtle tactics*. An example of this approach has been cited by Professor Gambrill from the University of California.

> A young executive assistant became very angry when one of her superiors belittled her, which often occurred in front of others. This situation had become so unpleasant that her superior was about to recommend her dismissal and she was thinking of resigning. She was instructed to wait for the next incident and then at the first opportunity, to take him aside, tell him with obvious embarrassment something to the effect that when he talks to her in that way, it 'turns her on', and then leave quickly before he could say anything. The client found the idea enormously funny. She stated that the very next day her superior's behaviour had changed and that he had been polite and easy to get along with since that time. She had not made the confession to him.

Training in Positive Expression

An aspect of social skill training which is often neglected in the literature is 'training in positive expression'. As one needs to be able to defend one's rights and express preferences appropriately, one should also be able to please other people (by offering compliments, showing affection, interest, etc.). Here are some examples. It might be useful to incorporate them into your rehearsal desensitization procedure.

—— How did you do it? Dieting takes real will power. I really wish I had your determination.
—— Hello. How are you?
—— How are things over there?
—— Your hair looks marvellous.

Here are three examples. First, a real life instance of positive expression has been reported by Dale Carnegie in *How to Win Friends and Influence People* as follows.

> I asked the information clerk in Radio City for the number of Henry Souvaine's office. Dressed in a neat uniform, he prided himself on the way he dispensed knowledge. Clearly and distinctly he replied: 'Henry Souvaine (pause) eighteenth floor, (pause) Room 1816.'
> I rushed for the elevator, then paused and went back and said, 'I want to congratulate you on the splendid way you answered my question. You were very clear and precise. You did it like an artist. And that's unusual.'

Beaming with pleasure, he told me why he made each pause, and precisely why each phrase was uttered as it was. My few words made him carry his necktie a bit higher; and as I shot up to the eighteenth floor, I got a feeling of having added a trifle to the sum total of human happiness that afternoon.

The second example goes as follows. The parents of one of a young couple visited the couple four times per year, staying each visit for about three weeks and taking over all household responsibilities during their stay. The husband was concerned that they would be hurt if their efforts were rejected.

This is what they did. They allowed the house to become dirty and the laundry to pile up prior to their next visit and to allow the parents to carry out all household chores, repairs, and responsibilities without any suggestion that they should not engage in these tasks. The parents cut the visit short and the father told his son that he (the son) and his wife were much too pampered, that they had become much too accustomed to being waited on and supported by the parents, and that it was now high time to behave in a more adult fashion and to become less dependent on them.

Here is the final example. A law clerk was constantly harassed during daily prolonged lectures by his superior (Mr J.). Since Mr J. was known to be hypochondriacal, he feigned a worried expression and interjected some statement relating to his health during the next lecture. Specifically, he stared at the left cheek of his superior. Almost immediately, Mr J. stopped short and irritably asked what was wrong, whereupon the client asked him if he felt well. The interview was abruptly terminated less than two minutes later. After one other such occasion, Mr J. avoided the client and the unpleasant interviews were at an end.

13.

The Way to Self-Confidence

The importance of self-confidence cannot be underestimated. It is, as Emerson said, 'the first secret of success'.

Yet, from universal human experience it is known that such an attitude is difficult to acquire. A person is more likely to doubt his own worth than to think of himself in positive terms.

The limiting nature of such self-doubt has been expressed by Alexander Dumas so well: 'A person who doubts himself is like a man who would enlist in the ranks of his enemies and bear arms against himself. He makes failure certain, by himself being the first person to be convinced of it.' Or, as Shakespeare put it, 'Our doubts are traitors making us lose the good we oft might win, by fearing to attempt.'

The step by step instruction to be outlined below will allow you to deal systematically with this self-defeating behaviour and to use self-hypnosis to help you achieve self-trust.

Step 1: Making Concrete Formulation of Goal
See Chapter 3. Additionally, the following goals are worth while noting, as they are specific to the problem at hand.

—— When I am speaking, I would like to be able to look directly at the person listening.
—— When I am giving my report, I would like to be able to speak eloquently.
—— I would like to feel good about myself more often.

Step 2: Gaining Access to the Unconscious
Use the procedures taught in Chapter 3 to put yourself into hypnotic state.

Step 3: Success Visualization and Self-suggestion (Positive Thinking)

Use the Success Visualization taught in Chapter 3. Additionally, you may give yourself the following suggestion several times per day.

The past will lose its power over me since I know that it cannot affect me unless I decide to honour it. I am greater than I thought.

Day by day, I will feed positive, happy thoughts into my mind and this will replace the negative self-defeating sentences I told myself in the past. I will be as happy as I make up my mind to be. I will think and act cheerfully, and I will be cheerful.

When I have any task to perform, I will think of it as easy. I will be able to rely upon my own efforts, to depend upon my own judgement, my own opinion. By virtue of being a human being, I have the ability to go beyond myself and rise above my conditions. Such words as 'difficult', 'I cannot', 'impossible' will disappear from my vocabulary; their place will be taken by this phrase 'It is easy and I can'. I will become truly human by defining myself in choices.

I will find myself and be myself, since no one else on earth is like me. No matter what happens, I will always be myself. I will do what I feel is the right thing to do.

Since I cannot possibly be anyone else, I will do those things that I enjoy doing rather than the things other people think I ought to do. I will set about doing things without worrying whether I do them perfectly, since I know that I have the right to make mistakes. I am a valuable worthwhile person because I am (insert your name), not because of how well I do something. Nevertheless, I will learn from my mistakes and become increasingly successful and competent.

I will be glad of the fact that I am something new in this world. With each passing day, I will make the most of what nature gave me. I will be what my experiences, my environment and my heredity have made me. For better or worse, I will cultivate my own little garden.

The power which resides in me is new in nature and no one but I know what I am capable of doing. Nor do I know until I have tried. It is not by the size that I win or I fail, but by my courage to be the best of whatever I am.

Step 4: The 'As If' Principle

Wake yourself up and strengthen the effect of Step 3 by using the 'As If' Principle taught in Chapter 3 and 13.

EPILOGUE: PERSISTENCE:

As with any other learning endeavour, you need to keep everlastingly at your goal. Continue to march forward despite some initial difficulty. Be like Abraham Lincoln. After he had been beaten by Stephen A. Douglas in the race for the U.S. senate, Lincoln admonished his followers not to 'give up after one nor one hundred defeats'. Capture the spirit of Rudyard Kipling. (A complete version is given in Chapter 15.)

If you can dream and not make dreams your master;
  If you can think and not make thoughts your aim;
If you can meet with triumph and disaster;
  And treat those two impostors just the same,

If you can force your heart, and nerve, and sinew
  To serve your turn long after they are gone;
And so hold on when there is nothing in you
  Except the will which says to them HOLD ON,

If you can fill the unforgiving minute
  With sixty seconds' worth of distance run,
Yours is the earth and everything that's in it,
  And, what is more, you'll be a man, my son.

14.

Ten Secret Techniques

In this chapter, I want to describe ten strategies which are usually hidden in the various professional journals and are therefore not accessible to the general public. This is the reason why I have called them *secret*. Strategies 1, 3, 6 and 9 are to be used as Step 3 (Self-suggestion), while the rest are to be used as Step 4 (The 'As If' Principle and 'In Real Life' Activity) in the model for the effective use of self-hypnosis.

1. Red Balloon Technique
This technique is indicated for those who have a great many negative feelings (gloom, unhappiness, depression, frustration, etc).

It proceeds as follows. Imagine yourself outdoors. The sky is blue and the weather is ideal. Near your feet there is a small container. Feel as vividly as possible all your negative feelings flowing into that container, until you are completely cleansed.

Next, go to a peg where a big red balloon is tethered. Loosen the red balloon from the peg, move across to the container and thread the free end of the cord through the handle in its lid. Let it go.

Watch the red balloon and the container rise in the air. As they become smaller and smaller, experience an ever-increasing feeling of happiness, which culminates in their disappearance.

Carry out this technique twice per day, and whenever you feel a need to change your feelings.

2. The 'As If' Principle
This technique is indicated for those who wish to change their personality, (to become more courageous, happier, etc).

It proceeds as follows. Conduct yourself as if you had already become your ideal self. Use all your will and imagination to the attainment of this goal.

The father of modern Psychology, Professor William James, taught this principle when he said,

> Action seems to follow feeling, but really action and feeling go together; and by regulating the action, which is under the more direct control of the will, we can indirectly regulate the feeling, which is not.
>
> Thus, the sovereign voluntary path to cheerfulness, if our spontaneous cheerfulness be lost, is to act as if it were already there. If such conduct does not make you feel cheerful, nothing else on that occasion can.
>
> So, to feel brave, act as if we were brave, use all of our will to that end, and a courage fit will very likely replace the fit of fear.

Similarly, the former U.S.A.'s president, T. Roosevelt wrote,

> When a boy, I read a passage in one of Marryat's books which always impressed me. In this passage, the captain of some small British man-of-war is explaining to the hero how to acquire the quality of fearlessness. He says that at the outset almost every man is frightened when he goes into action, but that the course to follow is for the man to keep such a grip on himself that he can act just as if he were not frightened. After this is kept up long enough, it changes from pretense to reality, and the man does in very fact become fearless by sheer dint of practising fearlessness when he does not feel it.
>
> This was the theory upon which I went. There were all kinds of things of which I was afraid at first, ranging from grizzly bears to 'mean' horses and gun-fighters; but by acting as if 'I' were not afraid, I gradually ceased to be afraid. Most men can have the same experience if they choose.

Also of Jesus Christ it is written,

> And Jesus answered them, 'Have faith in God. Truly, I say to you, whoever says to this mountain, "Be taken up and cast into the sea", and does not doubt in his heart, but believes that what he says will come to pass, it will be done for him. Therefore, I tell you, whatever you ask in prayer, believe that you have received it, and it will be yours.'

3. Barrier Smashing

This technique is indicated for those who feel that they cannot be all that they are capable of being, due to the pressure of unwanted public opinion.

It proceeds as follows. See the barrier as a brick wall.

Visualize yourself planting a demolition charge at the base of the wall, attaching it to a wire which you then unroll so that you are at a safe distance. Connect this to a plunger-controlled detonator and, looking at the wall, depress the plunger. The explosion is so powerful that nothing but rubble remains.

The visualization usually has an immediate effect. It uplifts the visualizer's spirit and gives him freedom to make more of himself.

Carry out this technique as often as it is necessary.

4. Thought Stopping and Thought Switching

This is an emergency technique which is extremely effective to get rid of an unwanted feeling, thought or desire.

It consists of three steps.

Step 1
Mentally get hold of the feeling, thought or desire by fully experiencing it for a few seconds.

Step 2
Suddenly – shout mentally '*stop*'; imagine a red traffic light flashing very very vividly in your mind's eye and tense some parts of your body slightly.

Step 3
Make an effort of the will to switch your attention either to a pleasant thought, image or activity.

One or two applications of this technique is usually sufficient to get rid of the unwanted feeling, thought or desire. If it returns, repeat the procedure.

5. The Mirror Exercise

This technique is indicated for those who wish to change their personality for the better (e.g. to get rid of 'stuttering'; to acquire 'discipline', etc).

In the night time, before retiring stand up in front of your mirror and gaze sincerely at your image for one minute. Experience the image fully as yours.

Next, define your ideal self with a single sentence only. For example, say with absolute seriousness, 'I am the best public speaker in the word.'

Simultaneously, force yourself to see the image as already transformed into your ideal self and experience this conviction fully for a few seconds.

Go to sleep immediately without doing anything else, so that the idea is deeply absorbed by your subconscious mind.

This is, admittedly, a slow technique. The transformation usually takes place after several months. But, once attained, it is not likely to reverse.

6. Energy Transfusion

This technique is indicated for those who feel physically tired or fatigued.

It proceeds as follows. Lie down in a comfortable place and start to deepen your breathing rate. Each time you breath in, imagine the infinite energy from the surrounding universe drawn into the nose, coursing down through the throat, heart and then solar plexus. As you breath out, feel the energy flowing into the tired parts of your body. At all times visualize the energy in the form of *white light*.

Continue for approximately ten minutes. Repeat as often as it is necessary.

Here is a similar method which has the added benefit of giving you psychic strength when you do not really know what is to be accomplished (you just want to improve).

Say to yourself the following.

My subconscious mind is all-powerful, far more powerful than my conscious mind. It never sleeps, it is continually working for my welfare, day and night, even if my conscious mind does not know it.

During my life, I am continually exposed to various things – good and bad. Naturally my conscious mind is eager to pick up the good. But, sometimes, my conscious mind does not know what to do or how to do it.

My subconscious mind, however, is continually absorbing the good – any time, any place, even if, due to ignorance, my conscious mind rejects it.

Now, go into the quiet of your own interior self, holding the thoughts,

I am one with the INFINITE POSITIVE ENERGY of my subconscious mind, which is the life of my life. In my own real nature,

I can admit of no illness or inferiority. I now open myself fully to the inflowing tide of this energy and it is now pouring in, and coursing through me.

Realize this so fully that you begin to feel a quickening and a warming glow imparted by the life forces to your body and mind. Then, say,

I believe that the life enhancing process is going on and I shall hold continually to it in my daily life. As I do so, there would be an ever-increasing feeling of conviction, of certainty, that the wish would be granted; that day by day, week after week, there would be a mounting feeling of intense, pleasurable tension, to the effect that some change is slowly, progressively taking place – within my mind and body – which would be fully realized at any chosen time or on the occasion of some special event.

7. Living One Day at a Time

This technique is indicated for those who are constantly depressed because of the inevitable hardships of life.

It can be summarized by the sentence which heads this section' Living one day at a time'. Or, to quote Sir William Osler: 'Live in day-tight compartments'.

The famous Indian dramatist, Kalidasa, has put the point accurately in his poem '*Salutation to the Dawn*'.

Look to this day!
For it is life, the very life of life.
In its brief course
Lie all the verities and realities of your existence:
The bliss of growth,
The glory of action,
The splendour of achievement.
For yesterday is but a dream
And tomorrow is only a vision,
But today well lived makes yesterday a *dream of happiness*
And every tomorrow a *vision of hope*.
Look well, therefore, to this day!
Such is the salutation to the dawn.

Ella Whieler Wilcox expresses similar thoughts.

With every rising of the sun,
Think of your life as just begun,
The past has shrived and buried deep
All yesterdays; there let them sleep.

Concern yourself with but today,
Woo it, and teach it to obey,
Your will and wish. Since time began
Today has been the friend of man;

But in his blindness and his sorrow,
He looks to yesterday and tomorrow.
You, and today! a soul sublime,
And the great pregnant hour of time,
With God himself to bind the twain!
Go forth, I say – attain, attain!
With God himself to bind the twain.

8. Ron Farmer's Emergency Techniques

Dr Ron Farmer is one of the Americans who brought 'Behaviour Modification' to Australia. Eight years ago, at the peak of his career as a lecturer in Psychology at the University of New South Wales, he suddenly found himself a victim of 'terror' episodes and soon found out that there was nothing psychologists and psychiatrists could do. Consequently, he disappeared to the countryside to find ways to help himself.

In his tape, '*The Nervous Breakthrough*' he describes three emergency techniques to deal with terror attacks.

Technique 1
It is well known that water is a powerful cleansing agent. Thus, each time you find yourself in the middle of terror episodes, wash yourself and think of nothing but the purification of your mind and body.

Technique 2
Draw a circle around you and repeat silently, 'Only the good shall enter'. This technique comes from the time of magic and has the power to repel negative influences.

Technique 3
This is the most powerful technique of all. Sit down in the position of the unborn baby in the womb.

In his tape, Dr Farmer reported a time during which he felt such a strong fear that he had to use the three techniques all at once. He washed himself many times, sat down on his bed and drew a circle around him with his finger. Then, he put technique three into practice and stayed in this position the whole night. When the morning came, Dr Farmer had enough energy to resume his normal activities.

9. Praying

The power of prayer is well understood by the greatest minds in the world.

'Trouble and perplexity drives us to prayer and prayer driveth away trouble and perplexity.' (Philip Mclanchthop)

'Lord, thou madest us for thyself, and we can find no rest till we find rest in thee.' (St Augustine)

'If God be for us, who can be against us?' (Romans 8:31)

'Prayer builds strength within against the stress of life.' (M. Aurelius)

'No man ever prayed without learning something.' (Emerson)

'Without prayer, I should have been a lunatic long ago.' (M. Gandhi)

There are at least three benefits to be derived from prayer. First, it will clarify your problems. As Charles Kettering put it, 'A problem clearly stated is a problem half solved.'

Second, in prayer one takes all his troubles to a power greater than oneself. It thus promotes a sense of sharing, the feeling that one is not alone. Prayer is a way of uplifting one's spirit, of transcending self.

Lastly, prayer, as any other sincere desire, is the first step towards action. As A. Carrell said, 'Prayer is also the most powerful form of energy that we can generate.'

Why not close this book right now, go to your bedroom, shut the door, kneel down and take your problem, whatever it may be, to God in prayer? Tell Him all about it, just as if He didn't know a thing. In the telling, be absolutely honest and sincere.

Next, believe that God will hear you and wait patiently for His answer. It may take hours, days or even weeks, but He certainly will answer you.

Then when He speaks to you, do what He tells you. It generally comes in the form of a sudden intuitive conviction that such and such a course of action is the one He wants you to take.

If you do not know how to pray, repeat the powerful passages from Psalm 27:14 and Psalm 23 silently and believingly.

> Don't be impatient. Wait for the Lord, and he will come and save you! Be brave, stout-hearted and courageous. Yes, wait and he will help you.

> Because the Lord is my Shepherd, I have everything I need!
> He lets me rest in the meadow grass and leads me beside the quiet streams. He restores my failing health. He helps me do what honours him the most.
> Even when walking through the dark valley of death I will not be afraid, for you are close beside me, guarding, guiding all the way.
> You provide delicious food for me in the presence of my enemies. You have welcomed me as your guest, blessings overflow.
> Your goodness and unfailing kindness shall be with me all my life, and afterwards I will live with you forever in your home.

10. Paradoxical Intention

This technique was designed by Professor Viktor E. Frankl from Vienna. It is indicated for all types of conditions in which performance anxiety is predominant.

Basically. it proceeds as follows. Make fun of your problem and try as hard as you can to make happen what you are afraid of. Thus, if you are a stutterer, try to demonstrate your stuttering capacity. If you are a blusher, try to become the greatest blusher in the world.

A few illustrations would probably clarify this point. The following case is reported by Dr Gerz from Connecticut Valley Hospital.

> Mrs L.K., aged 38 and married, suffered from a fear of dying of a heart attack because of attacks of tachycardia and severe palpitations. After she had suffered from this almost intolerable condition for several years, she decided one day 'not to give a damn anymore. I went into the yard and started digging', saying

to herself meanwhile, 'performing hard work is either going to kill me or not, but I am going to find out.' After she had worked for some time, she noticed that both her fear and the palpitations disappeared.

The following case was reported by Dr Viktor E. Frankl himself.

One of my American students who had to take an exam I was giving and, in this setting, explain paradoxical intention, resorted to the following autobiographical account. 'My stomach used to growl in the company of others. The more I tried to keep it from happening, the more it growled. Soon I started to take it for granted that it would be with me the rest of my life. I began to live with it – I laughed with others about it. Soon it disappeared.'

15.

Successful Strategies:
How I Solved My Problem

I continually receive testimonies from my clients and students about their successes. Most of them, I fear, are clear only to me and are therefore not suitable at all for publication. Several of a very small percentage which are self-explanatory, are presented in this chapter.

Case 1: Relaxation and Fear of Public Speaking
Patient: Female, 25 years old, university tutor (psychology)
Strategies used: Chapters 4 and 16.

I used to have a severe fear/anxiety about public speaking. Several weeks ago, I had been timetabled in my job to teach in that week for twelve hours. As that week approached my anxiety increased. The students were only two years younger than myself, I did not fully understand the material I was teaching and I felt that I would be ridiculed by the students for my lack of self-confidence.

During the days approaching the start of the lessons, I practised relaxation and one thing I found particularly helpful and meaningful was a repetition of the statement 'It doesn't matter if they don't like me.' Before and at the start of each lesson I would breathe deeply and repeat this statement.

Well, the outcome was that the week was great. I loved teaching. I was still a little bit nervous with some groups (I had six groups). In fact, I suppose I was nervous with them all at the start of each session, but as the session progressed I seemed to calm down. I realized that it did not matter at all how I appeared in front of these people. I am now taking two tutorial groups per week. One group I feel totally comfortable with (the effects of practice probably came into it with this group), and the other group I feel a bit uncomfortable with, mainly because they are a very unresponsive group and I have not been taking them for long.

I think that the main discovery I have made is that *it doesn't matter really how I look in front of people* and that *relaxation does do wonders if you practise*.

Case 2: How I Used Relaxation to Retain my Dignity
Patient: Male, 70 years old, retired lawyer.
Strategies used: Chapter 4

I have two boys who are inclined to argue at meal times. My usual reaction is to act as though I am in a temper and to shout at them. I found this affected me more than them and that my assumed (as I thought) temper became very real. This meant that I felt worse than they.

By relaxing before the meal and telling myself to remain calm I found that I was not nearly so upset and could handle the situation far more calmly and quietly and with much more dignity.

Case 3: How I Used Desensitization to Reduce Anxiety
Patient: Male, 36 years old, university student (final year).
Strategies used: Chapter 4.

During a group meeting of a 'Guidance and Counselling' course it was decided that each member should leave the group and while they were outside they would be discussed by the remaining members. This situation was anxiety-provoking and usually on returning, some anxiety-producing remark or action was made.

The following week, after all had been out and discussed we were to convey the comments of the group to the respective person.

I went out while the group formulated their ideal about me and, at first I felt confident that the situation would not break my resolve to be calm, but very soon nagging doubts about myself gave rise to the uncomforting sensation of anxiety. My stomach rose as it does when a lifts descends too quickly or an aeroplane hits an airport. There was no objective reason for anxiety; only the separation from the group, self-doubts and self-depreciation were the villains in this case. I could think of no reason to become anxious, but that was what I was becoming.

I applied the main principle of controlled desensitization, namely to take a deep breath, hold it, breathe out and say 'CALM', allowing a feeling of calmness and relaxation to flow throughout my body.

I felt that this blocked the anxiety and stopped it engulfing me – it didn't eliminate it, but it did alleviate its main effects.

I remained outside for perhaps ten minutes and when called in I was able to face the criticisms with some degree of equanimity.

Case 4: Relaxation and Insomnia

Patient: Female, 70 years old, retired school teacher.
Strategies used: Chapter 8.

I have found the relaxation exercise beneficial in overcoming insomnia. Before practising the exercise, I often lay awake for two or three hours during the night. I would next be worrying about everything and there would be no apparent reason for my insomnia – so after the wakefulness lasted for one-and-a-half to two hours I would switch on the lamp and read till I felt sleepy.

Since practising the exercise eight or nine weeks ago, there have *only* been *two occasions* when the exercise has failed to relax me and prevent insomnia.

Regards and thanks.

Case 5: Relaxation and Positive Thinking

Patient: Male, 38 years old, clerk (computing).
Strategies used: Chapters 4 and 16.

The moment had arrived. I heard my name being called. 'The next speaker will be Mr R.C.' My pulse quickened and a dry feeling came to my throat, also my knees felt weak. Then I remembered prior relaxation exercises and the suggestions I had been giving myself for the last two weeks.

I took several deep breaths and said 'CALM', a calmness filled my body and mind and I walked slowly to the front of the class to present my talk. I remembered the suggestions very clearly now and with each moment I became more confident.

The thoughts that filled my mind were:

—— You know your subject well and you are well prepared.
—— You are the most important person you know and you know you are capable of a presentation as good as any other person.
—— You are relaxing as you realize that tension will only spoil your performance.
—— You will look at the listeners and talk to them as easily as you have talked to each of them individually.

I took another three deep breaths and after a pause I began my presentation. I had gained everyone's attention and as I progressed I realized that they were interested and that the fears of three weeks ago had disappeared.

After the talk had finished I asked if there were any questions. After answering several questions I concluded my talk.

It had worked. I was successful – I realized, that any time I had to present a talk in the future that I would have no difficulty. Because of my success in the presentation, *I realized that within myself I had the ability to do whatever I wished to accomplish.*

Case 6: The Power of Love
Student: Female, 39 years old, housewife.
Strategies used: Own invention.

A few years ago the manager of my husband's department was a very difficult person to deal with. He was very negative and always made things as hard for the people in the department as he could. My husband took it personally and would come home very unhappy and even discouraged many times. I had just gotten into the 'Truth and New Thought' movement at the time and was learning some very interesting principles. I could see that my husband was returning the manager's negative vibrations and thoughts to him. I am sure each could feel the other's animosity.

One evening B. (my husband) and I sat down and discussed the situation and I suggested that when Mr O. was particularly bad that B. silently sent him love and see him in his mind as a kind person, ignoring the meanness.

B. was desperate and agreed to try it since he was in the verge of asking for a transfer. I worked with him and would see Mr O. as a loving person, one who perhaps had many problems that caused his unhappy actions. We used the affirmation 'He is Thine as I am Thine. Do that which will make peace between us'. We said this as often as possible during the day and before sleep.

The situation almost immediately began to improve. B. also learned that Mr O. was completely under the domination of a demanding wife at home and felt he had to assert himself at the office to boost his ego.

The best happening was that he and B. became friends as far as Mr O. could bear friendship. B. no longer took it all personally.

Case 7: The Great Value of Relaxation
Student: Female, 38 years old, receptionist.
Remarks: For a clear exposition of various relaxation procedures and their uses, see Chapters 3, 4, 8 and 12. This case also bears upon Chapter 9.

A recent incident has made me aware of the great value of relaxation. I had a long and painful telephone conversation with a young solicitor who stammered very badly throughout the entire conversation. I was becoming quite impatient because I was very busy at the time and he had telephoned me and interrupted my work. It was quite difficult to understand his speech and I found myself becoming tense with the strain. The conversation concerned a car accident claim with which I was unfortunately associated. Finally, after 20 minutes spent in this fashion, I was able to ascertain that he required me to return to the scene of the accident and take measurements and draw diagrams of the positions of the two vehicles, etc. When I agreed to do this and contact him again when I had the required information – which meant he *was able to relax* as he had conveyed to me what he required and I had agreed to do this – then he said to me lucidly, fluently and as clear as a bell, 'Thank you Mrs H. I will hear from you next week. Goodbye', *without the slightest trace of a stammer!* This was *simply because he had relaxed.*

Case 8: Choosing How I Feel

Patient: Female, 35 years old, homemaker (also temporary
   clerk and technical college student).

Strategies used: The 'As If' Principle (Chapter 14).

Several days ago I experienced an incident in which I was
aware of applying successfully the 'As-If' principle. B., my
husband, and I were both enjoying a relaxing time at home
after the children had gone to bed. Suddenly, B. remembered
something we had forgotten to do earlier in the day. It was
annoying that we had forgotten this and so B. did in fact
become very annoyed. Usually, I would join B. in his feelings
i.e. if he gets angry, so do I, if he gets depressed so do I, etc.
This night I was aware that B. was annoyed, but that I didn't
have to be annoyed also. I *consciously decided that I would be
relaxed and calm,* but at the same time allow B. to feel his
emotion of annoyance. The result was that B.'s annoyance
was short lived compared to if I had become annoyed also. We
were able to go back to having an enjoyable evening, free of
tension, whereas normally, if we had both got upset, that
would have been the end of any pleasant time. It would take
ages to get back to being relaxed. I felt really happy with
myself and B. said he noticed my different reaction and
thought it was very good.

Case 9: I Used Self-Hypnosis to Improve my Marital Life

Patient: Male, 42 years old, computer consultant.

Strategies used: Chapters 3 and 16.

For the last six months I have been suffering from severe
depression. Last year, I fell in love with a girl much younger
than myself and I was undecided as to whether to leave my
wife and family and go and live with her, or to stay with my
family. Although I knew that I would be happier (if only
temporarily) to leave my wife, I could see that she would be
very upset if I did leave her, (she in fact, had threatened
suicide), and I would be evading my responsibility to my
family. The indecision about the situation was very unsettling
and caused me much unhappiness. Eventually, the affair
ended, so that no decision had to be made after all. Since that
time I have felt regret at not having left my wife, since I
thought that my indecision contributed to the end of the affair.

This was one of the causes of my recent depression.

The other cause was that I felt that my relationship with my wife was empty and hollow. Although we did not quarrel very much outwardly, I secretly felt very resentful towards her. Travelling home from work daily, I used to get very tense at the thought of having to face another evening with her. After listening to the lecture 'As You Think, so Shall You Feel' and 'The Age-Old Wisdom that Will Change Your Life', I began to realize that my attitude was a *direct result of the limited way I had come to think*. Using hypnotic trance, I gave myself for a few weeks the following positive suggestions. 'What happened in the past is now over. At the time I acted in good faith and was true to my own inner feelings, so I have nothing to reproach myself about. It is not essential to my happiness that I love someone deeply. I can accept my wife with all her faults, and she can no longer cause in me feelings of guilt.'

Since I have used these suggestions, I have found myself with much more peace of mind, and my depression has ceased entirely. I can now derive positive enjoyment from my work, and at home I am much more pleasant to my wife and so we get on well together.

Case 10: Self-Monitoring and Work Performance
Patient: Male, 26 years old, marketing manager.
Strategies used: A portion of Chapter 3.

One of the principles which I applied extremely successfully was the three-step method to control problem behaviour.

One of my problems, which recently had caused me some concern is my laziness or – more accurately – lack of energy when I have to perform tasks that I have no interest in. The three-step method involved:

1. Specifying a goal that can be measured.
2. Monitoring behaviour.
3. Gradually moving towards the goal.

In actual fact, I didn't follow the instructions rigorously, although I did perform the three steps. My goal was to be able to cheerfully get through all the work I have to do. I started drafting the exact list of everything I had to do with priorities on each item. The monitoring stage was simply checking out what I had done. The gradual goal was to attack each project one at a time. *Improvement was 100 per cent and immediate.* From the first day my work output increased very significantly and – what's more – I felt very happy about it and not at all tired. I am now able to plan my working day very much better and get through much more work. I am also a lot happier about my job.

Case 11: The Energizing Power of My Place of Peace

Patient: Female, 35 years old, housewife (and mother).

Strategies used: Chapters 3, 4, 12 and her own invention.

Glossary: 'Place of peace' = an imaginary place into which this patient enters from time to time (in her mind) whenever she needs an extra energy (vitality) to help her handle various problems of living.

I was recently invited to a dinner party where my husband and I were to make up a party of six. I have always had a fear of any formal engagement. I lack self-confidence both in my education and appearance. I knew that it was very necessary for my husband to attend this dinner as a new job was going to be discussed. I had a week's warning and during that time I spent a great deal of time doing relaxation exercises and feeding myself positive thoughts. As I relaxed, I took myself to my 'place of peace'. While I was at peace I could do anything I wished or envied in others. I was able to tell myself that *there was no reason for me not to be a success.* I realized that I could be myself anywhere I went. Day by day in every way I was getting better and better. On the night of the dinner party I was surprised to find I was actually looking forward to it, even though I had never met any of the people there before. Before we went into the house, I closed my eyes for several seconds and went to my 'place of peace'. I saw myself as I wished to be. The evening turned out to be everything I hoped. It is a long long time since I have enjoyed myself so much. Several times during the evening I went to my 'place of peace'. My husband told me how proud he was of me and thanked me for making him feel so comfortable. He was given the job he so much wanted and I was thrilled to hear his new boss say that he was lucky to have a wife who was so natural and easy going. Any time I feel low now I am able to close my eyes and go to my 'place of peace'.

Case 12: I Forced Myself to Lose Control but ...

Patient: Female, 26 years old, nurse (also, part-time model, university student and housewife).

Strategies used: Chapters 3, 4, 12 and 14 especially 14 (Paradoxical Intention).

I have never approached giving a seminar with any degree of delight; indeed, talking in a group of friends above three or four in number has always been frightening. In one-to-one relationships I have never had any trouble, but even answering my name on a register at school would often have my heart beating fast. It was quite ridiculous, I was worrying about it and even chose my courses at university for small seminar numbers.

Last week I had to give two seminars following each other. Everyday I would do the self-control desensitization. I would imagine myself in the seminar room, sweating and with a thudding heart and then tell my body to relax, I would follow this with a few minutes meditation. I would repeat to myself, several times during the day rational statements, such as 'I'm very relaxed and very good at giving seminar papers – everyone will like my paper'. I carried out these exercises faithfully until I was quite fed up with them.

Eventually, the day of the seminar approached. I felt strangely calm, and was almost looking forward to it. Ah well, I thought, I will start shaking soon enough, my pulse rate will rise when I get to the room. I was prepared for this i.e. when I start to shake I will try to shake even more. Everyone will see how nervous I am, and that will be O.K. So what, everyone gets nervous.

When I got to the seminar room I was still not nervous. I couldn't understand it. Even when everyone quietened down and waited for me to begin. I waited for my hands to shake, but they didn't. In the end, I really did quite enjoy giving the paper.

The next day having another paper to give I didn't even think about it until I got to the room.

Case 13: Self-Hypnosis Gave Me a Clear Mind

Patient: Male, 46 years old, religious brother.
Strategies used: A modification of Chapter 3.

In the past two weeks, having reached the decision to apply for twelve months leave of absence from my religious community, I made a written application, stating my intention to my religious superior. In turn, I was asked to discuss my case at an appointed time. Having been given one hour's notice, I immediately made time to enter hypnotic trance using the following three steps:

1. Quieten mind and relax body and be comfortable.
2. Say with conviction 'I am going to enter hypnotic trance'.
3. Repeat 'cue word' three times; each time going deeper and deeper.

During this time I allowed my attention to centre on my situation and thus clarify my intention.

During the consultation which followed, I presented my case in a clear and concise manner and thus was in control of self and was not overcome by fear or tension which has happened when confronted with similar situations. Another observation made, was that I was satisfied and felt good about what I had said, rather than feeling that I should have said something else or in a different way.

Case 14: When I Assert Myself I do not Stutter

Student: Male, 28 years old, computer programmer.
Strategies used: Chapter 9.

An incident taught me the value of asserting oneself (talking in the offensive) for a severe stutterer like me. I was attending a conference in August 1977, but the person I was going with suddenly decided not to go. (He resigned instead and went overseas for a year.) This was about a month before the conference and it was left up to me to deliver a half hour seminar to a group of about 100 people, none of whom I knew.

I was awake until about 1 a.m. the night before, preparing my material for 9 a.m. The fateful moment came, and as I remember, it went over very well indeed. I was not really aware of my surroundings; it was as though I was lecturing to nobody at all.

I attributed this to my frame of mind at the time. The subject of the seminar concerned a product in competition with the same one that everybody else was using. It was actually a computer programme that competed with the one offered by the manufacturer of the computer, and the conference was arranged by the manufacturer for the benefit of its users. I imagined myself in the situation of telling them something, which they didn't really want to hear, but was forced to. (That is to say, *I spoke in the offensive.*)

Case 15: Zen Formula Plus Self Command 'Easy' Increased My Energy Considerably

Patient: Male, 49 years old, social worker.
Strategies used: Chapter 3, Zen philosophy.

Zen philosophy, very generously transposed, has helped me more than anything else, not only to gain moment by moment control of my life, but also to be more productive in the larger sea of life. 'Do what needs to be done, with no deliberate mind, without motive or thought of result.' I apply this principle to every task and to every learning experience. Several years ago I was called upon without notice to give the principal address at a very large gathering of people. Momentarily, I panicked; then, by mentally repeating my seemingly contradictory muddled Zen, I delivered a thirty minutes speech which was quoted verbatim in the press. My recent experiences in the study of self-hypnosis has greatly strengthened this kind of adaptability. Nowadays, having repeated my formula, I merrily say to myself, 'easy'. This invariably helps. I work harder but with little resistance, and switch from one activity to another almost without pause. In other words, suggestion plus philosophy have become behaviourally autonomous to a great extent.

Case 16: I Use Self-Hypnosis to Add Pleasure to My Life

Student: Female, 32 years old, librarian.
Strategies used: A modification of Chapter 3.
Glossary: Satori = enlightenment (awakening).

I use hypnosis as a source of enjoyment. I feel hypnosis can help me to integrate my personality, and I decided to try this, but I didn't want to force anything on my mind. That is to say, I didn't want to impose my will on my mind to force it into behaviour with no natural will or impulse behind it. I wanted my experiences to happen and develop naturally, and grow from the roots in my unconscious mind, and I wanted them to be pleasurable and helpful to me. How could I get my unconscious self to co-operate with my will in this? I decided to use hypnosis to prompt my unconscious mind to give me direct communications in the form of dreams. That is to say, I put myself into the hypnotic state and let myself drift into a dream-like state which I called hypnotic dream.

The first dream I had was reassuring. I dreamed I saw a message written on a wall in chalk which promised me 'Dreams will help you and you will achieve satori' (I was very surprised to read the 'satori' because consciously I scarcely know what it means). I was delighted with this message, because it showed me I was on the right track, had the co-operation of my whole mind, and I felt I was right to trust my unconscious mind. Since then I have had other dreams and met helpful characters who have promised to help me in my dreams and in my waking life. I have met a medicine man to help me keep my health, and a kind and gentle woman to help me best express my negative emotions. I feel I am growing. I greatly enjoy these dreams, and waking up from them is pleasurable too.

16.

The Age-Old Wisdom to Change Your Life

The famous quotations given below are to be used as STEP 3 (Self-suggestion) in the model for the effective use of self-hypnosis. To give you a clearer idea about the power of Self-suggestions and the rationale behind them, I have added an addendum (As You Think so Shall You Feel) to this chapter. Note that the practical exercises given there are to be used as Step 4 (In 'Real Life' Activity).

Ralph Waldo Emerson
> Don't waste life in doubts and fears; spend yourself on the work before you, well assured that the right performance of this hour's duties will be the best preparation for the hours or ages that follow it.

Abraham Lincoln
> Most folks are about as happy as they make up their minds to be.

Shakespeare
> Self-love my liege, is not as vile a sin as self-neglecting.

Edwin Markham
> For all your days prepare,
> And meet them ever alike;
> When you are the anvil, bear,
> When you are the hammer, strike.

Job 34:29
> When he giveth quietness, who then can make trouble.

Mark Twain
> I am an old man and have known a great many troubles, but most of them never happened.

Charles H. Spurgeon
> Many men owe the grandeur of their lives to their tremendous difficulties.

Confucius

The gem cannot be polished without friction, nor man perfected without trials.

Ralph Waldo Emerson

When it is dark enough, men see the stars.

Henry Wadsworth Longfellow

Not in the clamour of the crowded street,
Not in the shouts and plaudits of the throng,
But in ourselves are triumph and defeat.

Luke 21:19

In your patience possess ye your soul.

Isaiah 30:15

In quietness and in confidence shall be your strength.

Ralph Waldo Emerson

A man is relieved and gay when he has put his heart into his work and done his best.

Oliver Wendell Holmes

The great thing in the world is not so much where we stand, as in what direction we are moving.

Booker T. Washington

Success is to be measured not so much
by the position that one has reached
in life, as by the obstacles which one has
overcome while trying to succeed.

Matthew 17:20

For truly, I say to you, if you have faith as a grain of mustard seed, you will say to this mountain, 'Move from here to there', and it will move; and nothing will be impossible to you.

Henry Wadsworth Longfellow

When you get low in spirit and discouraged, remember this: the lowest ebb is the turn of the tide.

Washington Irving

Great minds have purposes, others have wishes. Little minds are tamed and subdued by misfortune; but great minds rise above them.

John 8:32

... and you will know the truth, and the truth will set you free.

Romans 12:12

Rejoice in the hope. Endure under tribulation. Persevere in prayer.

Psalm 18:2

The Lord is my rock, and my fortress and my deliverer,
My God, my rock, in whom I take refuge,

My shield, and the horn of my salvation, my stronghold.

Oscar Wilde

Nothing in the whole world is meaningless. Suffering, least of all.

William James

Be willing to have it so. Acceptance of what has happened is the first step to overcoming the consequence of any misfortune.

Anonymous

When we stop fighting the inevitable, we release energy which enables us to create a richer life.

Viktor E. Frankl

Being human is being always directed, and pointing, to something or someone other than oneself; to a meaning to fulfil or another human being to encounter, a cause to serve or a person to love. Only to the extent that someone is living out this self-transcendence of human existence, is he truly human or does he become his *true self*. He becomes so, not by concerning himself with his self's actualization, but by forgetting himself and giving himself, overlooking himself and focusing outward.

Anonymous

Try to bear lightly what needs must be.

Anonymous

God grant me the serenity
To accept the things I cannot change.
The courage to change the things I can,
And the wisdom to know the difference.

Rudyard Kipling

If you can keep your head when all about you
Are losing theirs and blaming it on you;
If you can trust yourself when all men doubt you
But make allowance for their doubting too;
If you can wait and not be tired by waiting,
Or being lied about, don't deal in lies,
Or being hated don't give way to hating,
And yet don't look too good, nor talk too wise;

If you can dream – and not make dreams your master;
If you can think – and not make thoughts your aim,
If you can meet with Triumph and Disaster
And treat those two impostors just the same;
If you can bear to hear the truth you've spoken
Twisted by knaves to make a trap for fools,
Or watch the things you gave your life to, broken,
And stoop and build 'em up with worn-out tools;

If you can make one help of all your winnings,
And risk it on one turn of pitch and toss
And lose, and start again at your beginnings
And never breathe a word about your loss;
If you can force your heart and nerve and sinew
To serve your turn long after they are gone,
And so hold on when there is nothing in you
Except the Will which says to them: 'Hold on!'

If you can talk with crowds and keep your virtue,
Or walk with Kings – nor lose the common touch,
If neither foes nor loving friends can hurt you,
If all men count with you, but none too much;
If you can fill the unforgiving minute
With sixty seconds' worth of distance run,
Yours is the earth and everything that's in it
And – which is more – you'll be a Man, my son!

Anonymous

We cannot change the inevitable, But, we can change ourselves.

Anonymous

By lifting up your heart you will transform the unavoidable suffering into a heroic and victorious achievement.

Viktor E. Frankl

Life is never lacking a meaning. To be sure, this is only understandable if we recognize that there is potential meaning to be found even beyond work and love. Certainly, we are used to discovering meaning in creating a work or doing a deed, or in experiencing something or encountering someone. But we must never forget that we may also find meaning in life, even when confronted with a hopeless situation as its helpless victim, when facing a fate that cannot be changed. For what then counts and matters is to bear witness to the uniquely human potential at its best, which is to transform a tragedy into a personal triumph, to turn one's predicament into a human achievement. When we are no longer able to change a situation – just think of an incurable disease, say, an inoperable cancer – we are challenged to change ourselves.

Anonymous

Knife sharpens on stone;
Man sharpens on man.

Anonymous

Self-cultivation has no other method:
Extract its essence from your fellow man.
Ten million living things
Have as many different words.

Do not see yourself as the centre of the universe,
Wide, good and beautiful.
Rather, seek the wisdom,
Goodness and beauty in others
That you may honour them everywhere.
Anonymous
If a man dwells on the past, he robs the present,
But if a man ignores the past
He may rob the future,
The seeds of our destiny are nourished
By the experiences of our past.

As You Think So Shall You Feel

Dr A. Ellis, the founder of Rational Emotive Therapy has argued that there is not a direct causal link between an external factor (A) and the emotional consequence (C), following it. Rather, A can produce C only via a certain 'inner dialogue' (B).

Take a simple example. David is deeply depressed after Anne has left him. Here, A = Anne has left David. C = depression. A can produce C because David has reasoned as follows, 'Anne has left me. It proves that I am absolutely no good with girls, now and forever. How awful!'

The same situation, however, can leave another character, John say, only with a slight feeling of disappointment. How could this be? Easy, as John has reasoned as follows: 'Too bad my girl friend has left me. But, there is no evidence whatsoever that my happiness is determined by my girl friend's love for me. Therefore, I will, from now on, devote my time and energy to win someone else's love, and, if I am lucky, I might find someone better.'

In a sense, a human being is responsible for the way he feels. This is what J.P. Sartre caught sight of when he said, 'A man is nothing else but what he makes of himself'. The same line of thought was expressed by the Stoic philosopher Epictetus almost 2,000 years ago, 'Men are disturbed not by things, but by the views which they take of them.'

At this point, an irresistible conclusion follows. If only the individual cares to think more logically and rationally, he can undermine his own disturbances. As Dr Ellis put it,

If people essentially become emotionally disturbed because they unthinkingly accept certain illogical premisses, or irrational ideas, then there is a good reason to believe that they can be somehow persuaded or taught to think more logically and rationally and thereby to undermine their own disturbances.

In the examples which follow, an emotional problem (P) is caused by an irrational inner dialogue (D). P can be removed if the person in question can be persuaded to change the content of his inner dialogue into a healthy one (A).

1. P: Feelings of anger, resentment, hostility and over-rebelliousness.

   D: It is essential to be understood, loved and approved of by others.

   A: It would be nice if everyone loves and understands me. But it is not a dire necessity for an adult to receive love or approval from all those who mean anything to him.

2. P: Feelings of inadequacy, worthlessness, insecurity, self-damnation, anxiety and depression.

   D: I must achieve competence and perfection in all my undertakings. My self worth is determined by them.

   A: I am a valuable, worth while person because I exist as a human being, not because of how well I do something.

3. P: Hostility towards women.

   D: Julie lets me down so badly. I will never trust another woman again as long as I live.

   A: I overgeneralize. There is no evidence whatsoever that all women are alike. A suitable partner may well come up sometime in the future.

4. P: I cannot experience orgasm.

   D: Sex is dirty.

   A: 'There is nothing either good or bad but thinking makes it so.' (Shakespeare).

5. P: A university student is extremely depressed after he has failed his examination.

   D: I absolutely must succeed at university. It is horrible that I have failed. I cannot stand my failure. I will always keep failing. I rate as a rotten person for failing so miserably.

   A: It would be nice to succeed at university and it is most unfortunate that I have failed to get what I want. Now let me see whether I can succeed next time; or, if I can't succeed at all, let me see how I can feel reasonably happy without the advantages of a university degree.

6. P: A man is extremely upset after he has been fired from his job.

   D: I am a worthless slob. I can't stand it. I wish I were dead. How can I face people now? What will everyone think of me?

   A: I am not a total failure. I have merely failed in a few specific situations. Because I am fallible does not mean that I am worthless, useless and a complete failure. After all, to err is only human.

7. P: A woman is unhappy and depressed because her son, who has married and gone overseas has not been writing to her.

   D: My son should be in constant touch with his mother who has sacrificed so much for him.

   A: My son's first loyalty is to his wife. As a mother, I no longer have the right to prescribe a code of conduct for him.

8. P: Feelings of low frustration tolerance, avoidance, self-pity, inertia.

   D: The universe must make things easy for me, give me what I want without too much trouble or annoyance; and I can't stand it when this terrible universe doesn't.

   A: There is no free lunch. Hard work is the necessary condition of success.

If you look closely at the eight examples above, you will realize that a mental sufferer suffers because he is not willing to let go of his 'mustness' attitude (i.e. the attitude that such and such is a must to one's happiness and therefore has to come to pass), and that the way to cure is the adoption of a 'relativistic' attitude (i.e. the attitude that it would indeed be nice if such and such happens, even though it is not a dire necessity).

This is what you can do. Write several rational statements down (e.g. the 'A' statements) on small index cards and place them by your toothbrush in your bathroom. Each time you go to brush your teeth, read the cards to yourself, emphatically and in random order. As new, relevant ideas occur to you, you may drop one or two statements and add others. After a week has passed, they usually begin to sink in.

If your problem is very pervasive, however, it would be wise to use the lengthy procedure to be outlined below.

Spend ten minutes per day writing down and reflecting on (not repeating parrot fashion) the answers to the following six questions. Repeat each answer several times till it is felt to be true.

Q1   What is the emotional problem I wish to eradicate?
       Illustrative answer: My depression, (which is due to John leaving me).

Q2   What is the cause of the problem? That is to say; what kind of nonsense have I been telling myself?
       IA: John must love me. I cannot live without him.

Q3   *What rational evidence do I have for this belief?*
       The answer to this question must be '*none*', since modern science has solidly established that nothing can be known with absolute certainty. As Bertrand Russell has stated: "Not to be absolutely certain is, I think, one of the essential things in rationality". Thus, an illustrative answer would be as follows: None. There is no empirical evidence whatsoever that John must return my love.

Q4   *What evidence exists of the falseness of this belief?*
       IA: (a) No law of nature exists which says that John must love me.
       (b) John's rejection will not kill me.
       (c) My happiness is not determined by John's love. I can find enjoyment in friendship, books, etc.

Q5   *What is the worst that could happen if I do not get what I think I must?*
       IA: (a) I would feel inconvenienced by still wanting love and looking for it elsewhere.
       (b) I might remain alone much of the time, which again would prove unpleasant.

After you have answered this question, prepare yourself mentally to accept the answers. This usually has the effect of bringing about a sense of mental release. As William James put it:

Be willing to have it so. Acceptance of what has

happened is the first step in overcoming the consequence of any misfortune.

Similarly, according to Lin Yutang:
True peace of mind comes from accepting the worst.

The same thought has been expressed by Shopenhauer in this way:
A good supply of resignation is of the first importance in providing for the journey of life.

Also, a Mother Goose rhyme says:
For every ailment under the sun,
There is a remedy, or there is none.
If there be one, try to find it,
If there be none, never mind it.

And finally, consider the beautiful words of St Teresa of Avila:
Lord,
Give me the courage,
To change what can be changed,
To accept what cannot be changed,
And the wisdom to know the difference.

Q6 *How can I make good use of my misfortune?*

IA: If John does not love me, I could devote more time and energy to winning someone else's love, and probably find someone better.

To motivate yourself to carry the procedure out consistently, you may use the principle of 'reward' and 'punishment'.

Select some activity that you highly enjoy and tend to do every day, e.g. watching TV, having a cup of coffee, reading the newspaper, having a short walk, etc. Use this activity as a reward by only allowing yourself to engage in it after you have practised for at least ten minutes that day. Otherwise, no reward.

Additionally, you may punish yourself every single day you do not practise for at least ten minutes, by making yourself perform some activity you find distinctly unpleasant, e.g. contributing to a cause you hate, ringing your mother-in-law, etc.

If your upsetting feelings do not change into positive ones overnight, do not get discouraged. Keep repeating the assignment with high spirits, day by day, until you do change these feelings. Don't give up. You create and control your feelings. You can change them.

Appendix 1

How to Use Your Time Effectively

I want to describe here four time-saving principles which, if they are faithfully obeyed, can be expected to increase your efficiency considerably. Principles 1, 2 and 4 are to be used as Step 4 (Inactivity), and the first 4 questions given under principle 3 (*What is the 'real' problem?* etc) can be used after Step 2 (the hypnotic state) has been accomplished, using the procedures given in Chapter 3. Other parts of this principle are to be used as Step 4.

Principle 1: Be Sure that Your Desk is Occupied only by those Papers which are Relevant to the Immediate Problem at Hand

This principle allows you to concentrate better (and therefore makes your work much easier and more accurate), since you are not worried by irrelevant items of a million things to do and no time to do them; (for instance, the mere sight of a desk littered with unanswered mail, reports and memoranda is enough to breed confusion, tension and worries). To put the point differently; the principle allows you (if feasible, of course), to settle your problems quickly, one by one. It keeps you from the disturbing sense of 'must', the unending stretch of things ahead that simply have to be done. It gives you peace of mind.

Principle 2: Make a List, Set Your Priorities and do Them in the Order of their Importance

Making lists and setting priorities are essential for effective time management. As Alan Lakein (the author of *How to Get Control of Your Time and Your Life*) put it: 'Making the right choices about how you will use your time is more important than doing efficiently whatever job happens to be around.'

Priorities are a highly personal matter and no ironclad rule can be given here. However, the following questions may act as a stimulus to *right choices*: What do I wish to accomplish? Is it a short term or a long term goal? How much time do I have? Any limitations? (personality, finance, etc).

Once you have set up your priorities clearly, the importance of doing them in the order of their importance becomes obvious. Our capacity (mental and physical) gradually diminishes as we proceed with our work. If the most important thing is not done first, there is a possibility that it will not be done at all. And this will be a disaster. The American poet, Carl Sandburg has expressed this point so well: 'Time is the coin of your life. It is the only coin you have and only you can determine how it will be spent. Be careful lest you let other people spend it for you.'

Occasionally, degree of importance is correlated with degree of difficulty, (i.e. the most important thing is also the most difficult). In such a case, if feasible, try to make use of your 'natural body cycle'. Let me explain what I mean. We all do undergo cyclic patterns of changes in arousal, approximately every 24 hours and these are called *Circadian rhythms*. Basically, what this means is that within a given 24-hour period, everyone will have a *peak* of arousal when they are most productive and alert and a *trough* when they are unalert, inactive and wish to sleep. The times of day when these peaks and troughs occur vary naturally between individuals and everyone has to find out his own cycle. Charles Luckman, the former president of the Pepsodent Company, for example, has said: 'As far back as I can remember, I have got up at five o-clock in the morning because I can think better then and plan my day to do things in the order of their importance.'

Principle 3: When You have a Problem, Solve It When You have the Facts Necessary to Make a Decision. Act upon the Decision Immediately.

In its most concrete form, this principle can be spelled out in four steps (expressed as four questions):

1. *What is the problem?*
   In answering this question, two things should be taken

into consideration. Firstly, if the problem is too big to tackle, it needs to be divided into sub-problems, which should be tackled, one by one, in the order of their importance (*see* Principle 2), using the *four steps* being outlined.

Secondly, the problem needs to be stated in as concrete and specific a way as possible. In other words, it is no good saying: 'I am very upset'; 'What a terrible creature!' Instead, say: 'How can I get my idea across to my boss?'; 'Whom shall I marry – Anne, Leonnie or Jenny?'

2. *What is the cause (background) of the problem?*
   That is to say, inquire into the conditions which lie at the root of the problem. A concise answer to this question will lead smoothly to question 3.

3. *What are the possible solutions to the problem?*
   This is basically a brainstorming question. Just relax, let your mind go wild and give rise to unusual ideas and solutions (various things you can do to attack the problem). Do not judge them. Criticism is absolutely barred at this time.

4. *What is the best solution?*
   This is an evaluation phase in which you list the various arguments for and against your possible choices and then pick up one or two best solutions. To help you in this endeavour, consider the following tips: (*a*) Draw on the previously achieved problem situations. (*b*) Use your past experience, organizing and reorganizing it to bear on the present problem. (*c*) Dramatize the problem situation; construct various hypothetical situations relevant to the problem. (*d*) Personal inquiry, reading, discussion with friends, and so on.

It would be a good idea to write down the answers to questions 1-4 as this will deepen your understanding of the problem and help you to proceed along an orderly logical path to a reasoned conclusion.

Immediately act on the decision. Then, depending on the outcome, you may wish to modify your action accordingly.

A rather similar approach has been reported by Frank Bettger, a friend of Dale Carnegie (in *How to Stop Worrying and Start Living*):

1. I asked myself first: 'Just what is the problem?' The problem was: that I was not getting high enough returns for the *staggering amount of calls* I was making.

2. I asked myself: 'What are the possible solutions?' I got out my record book for the last twelve months and studied the figures. I made an astounding discovery! Right there I discovered that 70 per cent of my sales had been closed on the very first interview! 23 per cent of my sales on the second interview! And only 7 per cent of my sales on the third, fourth, fifth, etc, interviews. In other words, I was *wasting fully* one half of my working day on a part of my business which was responsible for only 7 per cent of my sales!

3. What is the answer? I immediately cut out all visits beyond the second interview, and spent the extra time building up new prospects. In a very short time, I had almost doubled the cash value of every visit I made from a call!

The above-mentioned procedure assumes that the problem can be formulated clearly within a short span of time, and that the answers to questions 2-4 will pop into your mind quite readily. Occasionally, however, this is not the case. Someone may sincerely feel a problem, and yet consider that it is not capable of being defined with sufficient clarity. Or the problem may have been clearly formulated, but the answers to questions 3 and 4 will not come readily. In such a case, it would be wise to *draw on the power of your unconscious mind*, using the four steps outlined below:

1. *Preparation*

   Try as hard as you can to answer questions 1-4. Devote some hours to it. This exercise will set your unconscious mind going. (This is actually a truism since we all know that solutions to our problems usually turn up after a labour of thinking has been made.)

2. *Incubation*

   This is a turning-off process whereby the material is put aside. It does not mean, however, that the problem is completely forgotten. Rather, the problem should often be turned over in your mind in a leisurely, unhurried and non-demanding way. This process will activate your unconscious mind even further.

3. *Illumination*

   After a while (hours, days, weeks, depending on the

difficulty of the problem), you will get an *Aha* experience whereby the answers to questions 1-4 (or perhaps only question 4) emerge fully, or just partially in the mind. Illumination, or part thereof usually occurs in odd situations (e.g. while in the toilet, shower, etc.), and it needs to be noted immediately, or turned over in the mind until it becomes crystal clear. Otherwise, you may lose it forever. You need to wait a little longer until the illuminations form a coherent solution to your problem.

It is most important to remember here that while you wait for the illumination to come, your mind must not lose its *optimism*. Paradoxically, the way to *rapid illumination* is by allowing your unconscious mind to proceed at its own pace and time and having an *unconditional faith* in it.

4. *Testing*

As has been mentioned earlier, you need to act upon the illuminations as soon as they form a coherent solution to your problem. Then, depending on the outcome, you may wish to modify your action accordingly. Two remarks are probably in order here. Firstly, Dr H.E. Stanton, Director of the Higher Education Research and Advisory Centre at the University of Tasmania, has stated: "You will never be able to collect all the information bearing on your particular problems. In fact, if you continually postpone making a decision on the grounds that there may be still more information available which you have not yet secured, you run the risk of being like the gentleman in the Chinese proverb: 'He who deliberates fully before taking a step will spend his entire life on one leg.'" Secondly, as I see it, *testing* is the essence of *success*. Our success is determined by our ability and willingness to learn from our experience – to be *constructively* self-critical. As Sir Karl R. Popper, the great methodologist teaches (in *Conjectures and Refutations*):

The way in which knowledge progresses is by tentative solutions to our problems, by conjectures. Criticism of our conjectures is of decisive importance: by bringing out our mistakes, it makes us understand the difficulties of the problem which we are trying to solve. This is how we become better acquainted with our problem, and able to propose *more mature solutions*: ... As we learn from our mistakes, our knowledge grows. Since our knowledge can grow, there can be no reason here for despair of reason.

Dr J. Murphy (author of *The Power of Your Subconscious Mind*) had described a case which illustrates (to some extent) the procedure taught here:

About forty years ago or more, Dr F. Banting, a brilliant Canadian physician and surgeon, was concentrating his attention on the ravages of diabetes. At that time medical science offered no effective method of arresting the disease. Dr Banting spent considerable time experimenting and studying the international literature on the subject. One night he was exhausted and fell asleep. While asleep, his subconscious mind instructed him to extract the residue from the degenerated pancreatic duct of dogs. This was the origin of insulin which has helped millions of people.

You will note that Dr Banting had been consciously dwelling on the problem for some time seeking a solution, a way out, and his subconscious responded accordingly.

Principle 4: Learn to Organize, Deputize and Supervize

It is hard to delegate responsibilities to others. For instance, the danger of delegating responsibility to the wrong people is well known. But difficult as it is to delegate authority, the executive must do it if he does not want to be overwhelmed by details and confusion, with the consequent worry, tension and fatigue. I suggest you follow the tips given in the preceding section to help you pick up the right people.

Appendix 2

The Success Factors

In order to get what you want, you must pursue your goal single-mindedly and with *passion*. The father of modern psychology, Professor William James, has expressed this point beautifully: In almost any subject, your passion for the subject will save you. If you only care enough for a result, you will most certainly attain it. If you wish to be rich, you will be rich; if you wish to be learned, you will be learned; if you wish to be good, you will be good. Only you must, then, really wish these things and wish them with exclusiveness, and not wish at the same time a hundred other incompatible things just as strongly.'

Closely related to passion is *driving force* – the realization that you have not only rights but also responsibilities – that there is no gain without work. According to the speaker cited by A. Tack (founder of 'The Tack Organization'):

Anyone can be successful if he is prepared to pay a price for success. That doesn't mean that we all can become millionaires. It means that in our respective spheres we can achieve a measure of success. The shop assistant can become the shop manager; the salesman can become the district manager; the office manager can become the general manager; the shop owner can become the owner of a chain of shops. But always remember that the price you have to pay is a continual price. If you refuse to pay it you will not succeed, and then you will become jealous of the success of others. If you stop paying the price when you have achieved some success, then you will slip back. That is why some companies achieve success for years, and then profits begin to fall. It means that the driving force has gone, and the price is no longer being paid. Not more than one man in fifty will pay any price whatsoever to enable him to succeed. He is always demanding his rights, and forgetting his responsibility.

Passion and driving force simply cannot get off the ground without *courage*, which is the recognition that failure is a genuine possibility, and that absolute certainty is an illusion. That is what Sydney Smith had to say about courage:

> A great deal of talent is lost in the world for want of a little courage. Every day sends to their grave obscure men whom timidity prevented from making a first effort, who, if they could have been induced to begin, would in all probability have gone great lengths in the career of fame. The fact is, that to do anything in the world worth doing, we must not stand back shivering and thinking of the cold and danger, but *jump in and scramble through as well as we can*. It will not do to be perpetually calculating risks and adjusting nice changes; but at present, a man waits, and doubts, and consults his brother, and his particular friends, till one day he finds he is sixty years old and that he has lost so much time in consulting cousins and friends that he has no more time to follow their advice.

The effectiveness of passion, driving force and courage as ingredients of success (*success factors*) will be greatly enhanced if you visualize yourself as a success and act accordingly several times per day. As the late Elbert Hubbard put it:

> Whenever you go out of doors, draw the chin in, carry the crown of the head high and fill the lungs to the utmost; drink in the sunshine; greet your friends with a smile and put soul into every handclasp. Do not fear being misunderstood and do not waste a minute thinking about your enemies. Try to fix firmly in your mind what you would like to do, and then, without veering off course, you will move straight to the goal. Keep your mind on the great and splendid things you would like to do, and then, as the days go gliding by, you will find yourself unconsciously seizing upon the opportunities that are required for the fulfilment of your desire, just as the coral insect takes from the running tide the elements it needs. Picture in your mind the able, earnest, useful person you desire to be, and the thought you hold is hourly transforming you into that particular individual ... Thought is supreme. Preserve a right mental attitude – the attitude of courage, frankness and good cheer. To think rightly is to create. All things come through desire and every sincere prayer is answered. We become like that on which our hearts are fixed. Carry your chin in and the crown of your head high. We are gods in the chrysalis.

The spirit behind passion, driving force, courage and success attitude is the unbendable spirit called *persistence*. Persistence enables you to hold on when there is nothing in you except the will which says to them, '*Hold On*'. The poem by Calvin Coolidge, already quoted on page 64, illustrates this point well.

Adequate as they may seem, passion, driving force, courage, success attitude and persistence *are not sufficient*, as by themselves they remain a blind force. They need to be regulated by *open-mindedness* – the ability and willingness to learn from our errors, no matter how painful they may be. This is how Dale Carnegie put this success factor into practical use:

> I have a folder in my private filing cabinet marked "F.T.D." – short for "Fool things I have done". I put in that folder, written records of the fool things I have been guilty of.
>
> I can still recall some of the criticisms of Dale Carnegie (the name of an organization: *my note*) that I put in my "F.T.D." folder fifteen years ago. If I had been utterly honest with myself, I would now have a filing cabinet bursting out at the seams with these "F.T.D." memos.
>
> When I get out my "F.T.D." folders and re-read the criticisms I have written of myself, they help me deal with the *toughest* problem I shall ever face: the management of Dale Carnegie. (*How to Stop Worrying and Start Living*.)

I suggest you put this article in a strategic place in your house or office and read it once a week. As you do so, try to recapture the spirits of the various sages cited; and, using them as your weapon, carry out your plans. You will find that the more you reflect on the essence of this article, the more profoundly you will understand the significance of the six success factors mentioned above (*passion, driving force, courage, success attitude, persistence* and *open-mindedness*), and the more effectively you will be able to apply them in your daily life. (This reflection can be used in the context of self-hypnosis, by first putting yourself under the hypnotic state, using the procedures given in Chapter 3 and then carrying it out while under it.) If you follow this tip faithfully, you may take comfort in William James' promise:

> Let no youth have any anxiety about the upshot of his education,

whatever the line of it may be. If he keeps faithfully busy each hour of the working day, he may safely leave the final result to itself. He can, with perfect certainty, count on waking up some fine morning to find himself one of the competent ones of his generation, in whatever pursuit he may have singled out.

We may make it more general:

Let no one have any anxiety about the upshot of his effort, whatever it is. If he keeps faithfully busy each hour of the working day he may safely leave the final result to itself. He can, with perfect certainty, count on waking up some fine morning to find himself a success, in whatever pursuit he may have singled out.

I have filled this article with quite a few highly selective citations, which have proved useful to my clients, students and myself. Perhaps I may end it with another quotation.

Success, for any sane adult, is exactly equivalent to doing his best. What that best may be, what its farthest reaches may include, we can discover only by *freeing ourselves from the will to fail*.

(Dorothea Brand)

Good luck.

Further Reading

Abelow, D., *Total Sex*, Ace Books, 1976.

Benson, H., *The Relaxation Response*, Collins, 1977.

Binder, V. and H. and Rimland, B., *Modern Therapies*, New Jersey: Prentice Hall, 1976.

Bloomfield, H.H.; Cain, M.P.; and Jaffee, D.T., *Transcendental Meditation*, London: Unwin Paperbacks, 1978.

Carnegie, D., *The Quick and Easy Way to Effective Speaking*, World's Work, 1962.

Carnegie, D., *How to Stop Worrying and Start Living*. World's Work, 1962.

Carnegie, D., *How to Win Friends and Influence People*, World's Work, 1953.

Cloud, J.M., *The Healthscription*, California; Holistic Health and Nutrition, 1977.

Ellis, A. and Harper, R.A., *A New Guide to Rational Living*, California: Wilshire Book Company, 1975. (Distributed by Thorsons Publishers, Wellingborough.)

Frankl, V.E., *Man's Search for Meaning*, Hodder and Stoughton, 1977.

Frankl, V.E., *Psychotherapy and Existentialism: Selected Papers on Logotherapy*, Penguin, 1973.

Frankl, V.E., *The Unheard Cry for Meaning: Psychotherapy and Humanism*, New York: Simon and Schuster, 1978.

Karbo, J., *The Lazy Man's Way to Riches*, California, 1973.

Ladell, R.M., *Overcoming Stammering*, Thorsons Publishers, Wellingborough, 1977.

Lamott, K., *Escape from Stress*, New York: G.P. Putnam's Sons, 1974.

Maltz, M., *The Magic Power of Self Image Psychology*, New York: Prentice-Hall, 1964.

Meares, A., *The Wealth Within*, Melbourne: Hill of Content, 1978.

Murphy, J., *The Power of Your Subconscious Mind*. New Jersey: Prentice-Hall, 1963.

Peale, N.V., *Norman Vincent Peale's Treasury of Courage and Confidence*, London: Unwin Books, 1973.

Rathus, S.A., and Nevid, J.S., *BT: Strategies for Solving Problems in Living*, New York: Doubleday and Company, 1977.

Reader's Digest Family Health Guide. Reader's Digest Services, Sydney, 1979.

Reed, S., *The Miracle of Psycho-command Power.* New York: Parker Publishing, 1972.

Sackheim, M., *How to Advertise Yourself*, MacMillan Publishing, 1978.

Sharpe , R. and Lewis, D., *The Success Factor: How to be Who You Want to be*, Pan Books, 1977.

Stanton, H.E., *The Plus Factor*, Fontana, Collins, 1979.

Taylor, R.B., *Dr Taylor's Self-Help Medical Guide*, New American Library, 1977.

Tohei, K., *Aikido in Daily Life*, Tokyo: Japan Publications Inc., 1974.